★✦★✦★✦★✦★✦★✦★✦★✦★✦

BASEBALL SUPERSTARS

Albert Pujols

★✦★✦★✦★✦★✦★✦★✦★✦★✦

Hank Aaron

Johnny Damon

Derek Jeter

Albert Pujols

Jackie Robinson

Ichiro Suzuki

✳ ✶ ✳ ✶ ✳ ✶ ✳ ✶ ✳ ✶ ✳ ✶ ✳ ✶ ✳ ✶ ✳ ✶ ✳

BASEBALL SUPERSTARS

Albert Pujols

Dennis Abrams

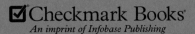

Checkmark Books®
An imprint of Infobase Publishing

✳ ✶ ✳ ✶ ✳ ✶ ✳ ✶ ✳ ✶ ✳ ✶ ✳ ✶ ✳ ✶ ✳ ✶ ✳

ALBERT PUJOLS

Checkmark Books
An imprint of Infobase Publishing
132 West 31st Street
New York, N.Y. 10001

Library of Congress Cataloging-in-Publication Data
Albert Pujols / Dennis Abrams.
    p. cm. — (Baseball superstars)
  Includes bibliographical references and index.
  ISBN 978-0-7910-9600-0 (hardcover)—ISBN 978-0-7910-9847-9 (pbk)
  1. Pujols, Albert, 1980- 2. Baseball players—United States—Biography. 3. Baseball players—Dominican Republic—Biography. 4. St. Louis Cardinals (Baseball team)
I. Title. II. Series.
  GV965.P85A37 2008
  796.357092—dc22
  [B]   2007029054

Checkmark Books are available at special discounts when purchased in bulk quantities for businesses, associations, institutions, or sales promotions. Please call our Special Sales Department in New York at (212) 967-8800 or (800) 322-8755.

You can find Chelsea House on the World Wide Web at http://www.chelseahouse.com

Series design by Erik Lindstrom
Cover design by Ben Peterson

Printed in the United States of America

Bang EJB 10 9 8 7 6 5 4 3 2 1

This book is printed on acid-free paper.

All links and Web addresses were checked and verified to be correct at the time of publication. Because of the dynamic nature of the Web, some addresses and links may have changed since publication and may no longer be valid.

CONTENTS

1

The Sound of Power

Let's begin with the sound of a bat hitting a baseball. Nothing is as distinctive as the sound of a well-hit ball coming off the sweet spot of a wooden bat. It is a sound that rouses baseball fans everywhere to stand up in excited anticipation of runs about to be scored. It can send fielders scurrying in one direction or another, trying to get a jump on the ball. It also tells the catcher, still in his squat, that the last pitch he called was probably a huge mistake. Today in Major League Baseball, nobody produces that distinctive "thwack" as consistently as Albert Pujols, the first baseman for the St. Louis Cardinals.

Anyone who truly knows baseball can tell just from the sound of contact almost exactly what kind of hit it is going to be. As Jim Hunter, the voice of the Baltimore Orioles on radio station WBAL, said, "When you're at a ball game and a guy gets good wood on the ball, there's a sound that it makes that kind of reverberates throughout the ballpark. It's almost a violent sound. You can tell when that occurs, as opposed to when a guy just puts the ball in play."

Dr. Robert Adair, a Yale physicist and author of the paper "The Crack of the Bat: The Acoustics of the Bat Hitting the Ball," agrees. He argues that the crack of a well-hit ball is not just sharper and louder than the sound made when a ball hits off the end of the bat or off its handle. Adair says it is a completely different sound altogether.

He says that, when the bat is struck at most points, it vibrates in a way similar to a guitar string, with waves too minuscule for the human eye to see. Those vibrations (at frequencies around 170 oscillations per second or higher) are what sting the batter's hands when the ball is not hit solidly and generate the "thud" sound that tells outfielders to run in closer, knowing that the ball is not going deep.

By contrast, that distinctive "crack" is caused by the ball being hit so hard that it literally flattens and wraps itself around the bat, if only for less than a thousandth of a second. Although the ball always flattens a bit on contact, the effect is slight unless the ball almost directly hits the bat's sweet spot. When that happens, the bat's vibration is kept to a minimum and the energy is transferred to the ball, resulting in a powerful hit. As Dr. Adair said, "If it's a crack, you know the ball is hit pretty hard, and you'd better start running backward."

Even as a teenager playing high school baseball in Independence, Missouri, Albert Pujols hit the ball in a way that sounded different from other kids' hits. His was more solid, more of a "whack." A sound of clean, pure power. It sounded as if a man were hitting the ball, not an inexperienced, young player. This difference in sound was noticed again when Pujols was in junior college. His coach at the time, Marty Kilgore, is quoted as saying, "You don't hear that kind of explosion often."

The distinctive "thwack" that is heard when the sweet spot of a bat connects with a pitch is a familiar sound when Albert Pujols, of the St. Louis Cardinals, is at the plate. Here, he pounded out a two-run double in a game on June 13, 2007, against the Kansas City Royals.

Then again, players like Albert Pujols do not come along that often, either. In just seven seasons of Major League Baseball, he has proven himself to be one of the finest players currently in the game, and he is on track to establish himself as one of baseball's all-time greatest players.

Consider the following numbers. He is the first major-league player since Ted Williams to get 100 runs batted in or better in each of his first seven seasons. He is the first player in Major League Baseball history to hit 30 home runs or better in each of his first seven seasons. He is the youngest player to hit 250 home runs. He is a Gold Glove winner for his fielding ability. He is the real deal, the complete package.

Former Cardinals hitting coach Mike Easler said about Pujols, "He has a passion for the game, a love for the game. You can see it. You can sense it. He's got natural God-given ability. A natural baseball player. A warrior. The man is good at every little thing he does."

Although Pujols may be a "natural" player, blessed with all the natural talent it takes to play the game, he is constantly striving to improve himself and his playing abilities. He works hard and trains hard, always looking for ways to polish his swing, outsmart a pitcher, or become a better fielder. For Pujols, playing baseball is a continuous learning process. And as great a player as he is, he is not afraid to ask a coach for advice.

Pujols himself said, "I'm a really smart player. If you tell me something, I get it quickly. If there is something wrong with my hitting, tell me what's wrong and I'll pick it up right away. That's the best thing I have going for me, my ability to listen to a coach and fix what I'm doing wrong."

His desire to be the best extends far beyond the baseball diamond. Pujols wants to be the best at everything he does. The best husband. The best father. The best community leader. The best teammate. And yes, the best hitter in all of baseball.

Unlike many other baseball superstars, however, he is not in it for his own personal glory. He is, above all else, a team player whose goal, whose very reason for playing, is to help his team reach the World Series and win the championship. To Pujols, no matter how good a season he has had, it is not a "great" year if he is at home in October watching the Series on television.

ROOTS

In many ways, it is remarkable that Albert Pujols has come as far as he has in so short a period of time. Born in the Dominican Republic to a poor family, raised largely by his grandmother, he and his family moved to the United States when he was just 16 years old to search for a better life. A star on his high school baseball team, he was a relatively unknown junior-college player when he became a thirteenth-round draft pick by the St. Louis Cardinals.

He played a remarkably small number of games at the Class A minor-league level before making the Cardinals' lineup in 2001 as a 21-year-old rookie. Observers during his first year of spring training were stunned by his talent but still had serious questions about his viability as a professional ballplayer. Could someone so young, so untested, so inexperienced make it in the high-pressure world of the majors?

Pujols quickly silenced many of the doubters. Even after his tremendous rookie year, though, some still wondered if he was just a "flash in the pan." Many players who were impressive in their first year faded quickly and were soon forgotten. Not Albert Pujols. His second season was so good that he finished just behind Barry Bonds in the voting for the National League Most Valuable Player award. With that, it became apparent to nearly everybody that, barring injury, Pujols would be a major baseball star for years to come.

As former St. Louis Cardinal and current broadcaster Mike Shannon said, quoted in *Albert the Great: The Albert Pujols Story*, "If he stays healthy and keeps performing like he's performing, which you expect, he's going to keep breaking records

☆ ☆ ☆ ☆ ☆ ☆

BARRY BONDS

If Albert Pujols has been compared to just one still-active baseball player throughout his career, it is his undeclared rival, Barry Bonds.

Barry Lamar Bonds was born on July 24, 1964, in Riverside, California. He is the son of former Major League Baseball All-Star Bobby Bonds and the godson of Hall of Famer Willie Mays. He is best known for being one of baseball's greatest power hitters, holding a number of records, including the most home runs in a single season, 73, a record he set in 2001.

On August 7, 2007, Bonds hit his 756th career home run to break Hank Aaron's record of 755. Through the end of the 2007 season, Bonds is first in career home runs (762), career walks (2,558), and intentional walks (688). Bonds also ranks second in extra-base hits (1,440), third in at-bats per home run (12.90), sixth in slugging percentage (.607), and fifth in RBIs (1,996).

He also leads all active players in home runs, RBIs, walks, on-base percentage (.444), runs (2,227), games (2,986), at-bats per home run, and total bases (5,976). Bonds has been compared with some of the game's all-time greatest hitters, including Ted Williams, Hank Aaron, Babe Ruth, Rogers Hornsby, and Ty Cobb.

In the last few years, though, his career has been somewhat overshadowed by the controversy surrounding his alleged steroid use. Although steroids were not outlawed by Major League Baseball at the time Bonds is alleged to have taken them, they were illegal in the United States without a prescription. For many people, because of the allegations of having taken performance-enhancing drugs (which Bonds denies), Bonds's achievements will always be under suspicion.

and do things that nobody's done before." So far, his prediction has come true.

But think about the odds against anyone making it as a baseball player. Think about all the people who play baseball in Little League or high school or college. Of all of those people, only about 1,500 young baseball players are signed by a Major League Baseball team each year. Of those 1,500 players, the vast majority will spend their careers playing in the minor leagues. Only a very small number will ever make it all the way to the majors. And of that number, only a tiny handful will thrive and become baseball stars, their names known and their achievements praised and argued about by baseball fans nationwide. Albert Pujols is one of those select few.

What is it that makes him so special? How did he prepare himself for a career in baseball? How does he balance the demands of professional baseball with those of family and religion? How does he try to make a difference in the world? What is it that makes Albert Pujols the man that he is?

Dominican Beginnings

Albert Pujols was born José Alberto Pujols on January 16, 1980, in Santo Domingo, the capital city of the Dominican Republic. In many ways, Albert was destined to play baseball. His father, Bienvenido, had been a star pitcher in the Dominican Republic and was well-known throughout the country. In any case, being born Dominican was almost enough, in and of itself, to propel any boy into a career in baseball, for it seems no country loves baseball as much as the Dominican Republic.

It has been said that baseball in the Dominican Republic is more than just a sport. Ask any Dominican what makes him most proud, and he will read you a list of ballplayers. No matter where you go in the country, you will find a baseball stadium or park, even in the poorest of towns.

And make no mistake about it—the Dominican Republic, a small nation that shares the Caribbean island of Hispaniola with Haiti, is a poor country, with 25 percent of the people living below the poverty level. For those kids growing up poor, baseball is a way out, offering an escape from poverty and a chance for a better life. They can recite the names of all the Dominicans who have left the country and become superstars in American baseball—Sammy Sosa, Pedro Martínez, Manny Ramírez, the list goes on and on. They are convinced that, if all those before them could make it, they too can become professional baseball players.

How can they not believe it? As of 2006, about 30 percent of all Major League Baseball players were of Latin American origin. One in 10 major-league players is from the Dominican Republic. But even though the training and recruitment of quality baseball players for the American market is a vital part of the Dominican economy, sugar is still the country's main crop, and it is in the sugar-mill towns that baseball took root.

Dominican and American mill owners approved of the sport and encouraged their workers to participate more than 100 years ago. The six-month dead season, when sugarcane requires minimum maintenance and the workers were unemployed, helped contribute to the development of baseball in the country. Soon, championships were set up pitting one sugar mill against another.

Four professional teams were founded in the early part of the twentieth century, and they eventually formed the Dominican Winter Baseball League, which now consists of six teams spread across the Dominican Republic. Since 1949, the winter-league winners of several Caribbean-area nations have met in the "Serie del Caribe" to determine the Caribbean championship. Baseball fans in the Dominican Republic root for their favorite Dominican teams as avidly as Americans do for their home teams.

Baseball is a popular sport in the Dominican Republic, and many young boys aspire to play in the major leagues, seeing the game as a way to escape poverty and improve their families' lives. Here, 12- and 13-year-olds play baseball at the Complejo Deportivo baseball camp in San Pedro de Macorís—a small town that has sent many players to the big leagues, including Sammy Sosa.

The recruitment of young baseball players has become a year-round job in the Dominican Republic. More than 20 major-league teams have training camps there for prospective players. Scouts from these teams are sent to hold tryouts throughout the nation. Those who are lucky enough to make the camps are usually young boys ages 17 and 18. At the camps, they are housed, fed, and taught baseball. The average player makes about $800 a month. In a country where the average income per capita is only about $7,600 a year, this is an enormous amount of money for any family.

Of those who make it to the team camps, only a small number ever reach the big leagues in the United States, but enough do so to inspire the dreams of many young Dominicans. They read about the exploits of their hometown heroes in the United States and dream of someday following them there. Also, these star players often come "home" to the Dominican Republic during the winter season. Escaping the cold of the American winter, they settle into large new houses that they have built for themselves and their families. People who can barely afford to buy food see New York Mets pitcher Pedro Martínez driving his yellow Ferrari and cannot help but think that, if he has made it, so could they.

"Kids over there play baseball from the time they can walk," said Bill Stoneman, the general manager of the Los Angeles Angels of Anaheim, as cited on the *Colonial Zone Dominican Republic* Web site. "They play barefoot, they play scantily clad, they play with things you wouldn't call a baseball. But they're playing baseball a lot more than American or Canadian kids. So it would make sense that a lot more of them are signing pro contracts."

Young kids in the Dominican Republic are crafty at finding ways to play baseball with poor or nonexistent equipment. Kids use milk cartons for gloves. They use a wadded-up cloth for a ball. They play using nothing more than a stick and a plastic cap from a large water bottle. They play baseball in the street, dodging traffic. They play baseball in a cleared sugarcane field. They play baseball on the beach. Albert Pujols was one of those kids.

GROWING UP POOR

Albert's father, Bienvenido, was often away from home looking for work. Because of this, Albert and his brothers and sisters were primarily raised by their grandmother, America. America had 11 children of her own, and many of Albert's aunts and uncles lived at the family home with them as well. (Albert's mother left when he was 3.)

According to several accounts, the family was nearly "dirt poor" and lived in a communal setting that was more like a camp site. Without the help of government-assistance programs, it seems doubtful that the family would have survived.

Despite his bleak surroundings, Albert grew up remarkably happy and well-adjusted. Most of the credit can be given to his grandmother, America. Loving and kind, she treated him as if he were her own son. She passed along to him her own strict code of ethics and her deep religious beliefs, both of which he holds strongly to this day.

Although Albert did not get to spend a great deal of time with his father, he knew from an early age that he wanted to follow in his footsteps and have a career in baseball. Indeed, from the time Albert could walk, he had his father's passion for baseball. As he once said, quoted in *Albert Pujols* by Jeff Savage, "I used to wear his uniform whenever I could. I wanted to be like him."

By the time he was six years old, Albert was playing baseball every day on the dusty fields outside his home in Santo Domingo, using nothing more than sticks and balls. He remembers playing catch using a lime and, like many others, making his mitt out of an old cardboard milk carton.

He would practice for hours every day. Even then, he knew that baseball offered the best chance for a better life for him and his family. As he said in Jeff Savage's *Albert Pujols,* "I knew if I wanted anything more, I'd have to work harder at it."

Whenever he had a chance, he would go along with his father to watch him play in the Dominican leagues. When he was not playing baseball or watching his father play, he would be watching baseball on television. Games featuring the Atlanta Braves were the easiest for him to find, but he never had a particular favorite team as a youngster.

As a boy, Albert Pujols sought to learn about pioneering Latino players in the major leagues, like Roberto Clemente, shown here in a 1957 portrait. Clemente played 18 seasons with the Pittsburgh Pirates, leading the team to two World Series victories. He died in a plane crash in 1972 as he was transporting aid to victims of an earthquake in Nicaragua.

Instead, his attention was focused on other Latin American players, like Sammy Sosa, Raúl Mondesí, and Julio Franco, his favorite player. All of these players had grown up in the Dominican Republic. If they could make it, Albert was certain, so he could he.

Albert's passion for all things baseball showed in his fascination with the sport's past. He was interested in learning all he could about baseball history and in learning about earlier Latin American baseball stars, like Roberto Clemente, Tony Pérez, and Juan Marichal. They became role models for Albert, proving to him that Latin American ballplayers could become stars in the American major leagues.

☆ ☆ ☆ ☆ ☆

ROBERTO CLEMENTE

One of Albert Pujols's heroes when he was growing up was Roberto Clemente. He was not alone in his feelings. For many, Clemente represents the best of what an athlete can be, and he was a hero to people worldwide, regardless of their interest in baseball.

Born in Carolina, Puerto Rico, Clemente was perhaps the first Latino baseball player to achieve across-the-board popularity. He was known for his powerful throwing arm—broadcaster Vin Scully once said that "Clemente could field the ball in New York and throw out a guy in Pennsylvania." He won 12 Gold Glove Awards for his outstanding defense in right field, tying a record held by Willie Mays. He reportedly could throw out a runner from his knees, and he recorded 266 outfield assists during his legendary career.

Also known for his prowess at the plate, he is renowned for being the only player to score a walk-off, inside-the-park grand slam—against the Chicago Cubs in July 1956. Playing his entire

By the time Albert was in his teens, his baseball talent became apparent to anyone who watched him play. He displayed enough raw talent that he began to receive the attention of scouts, who invited him to try out at the baseball camps sponsored by American major-league teams. It was the invitation that all young Dominican baseball players hoped for, the first step to playing in the big leagues.

DISAPPOINTMENT

Unfortunately for Albert, it was a step he probably was not ready or prepared to take. Despite getting invited to camps held by the Florida Marlins and the Oakland A's, Albert did

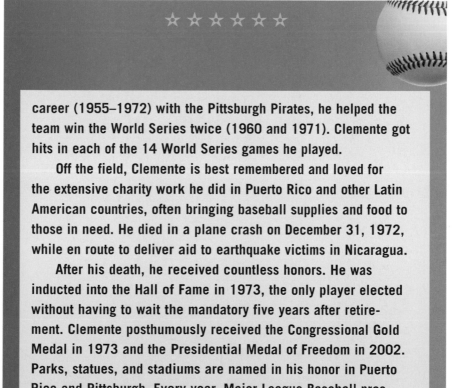

★ ★ ★ ★ ★

career (1955–1972) with the Pittsburgh Pirates, he helped the team win the World Series twice (1960 and 1971). Clemente got hits in each of the 14 World Series games he played.

Off the field, Clemente is best remembered and loved for the extensive charity work he did in Puerto Rico and other Latin American countries, often bringing baseball supplies and food to those in need. He died in a plane crash on December 31, 1972, while en route to deliver aid to earthquake victims in Nicaragua.

After his death, he received countless honors. He was inducted into the Hall of Fame in 1973, the only player elected without having to wait the mandatory five years after retirement. Clemente posthumously received the Congressional Gold Medal in 1973 and the Presidential Medal of Freedom in 2002. Parks, statues, and stadiums are named in his honor in Puerto Rico and Pittsburgh. Every year, Major League Baseball presents the Roberto Clemente Award to the player who best follows Clemente's example in humanitarian work.

not demonstrate enough skill and talent to win a minor-league contract from either team. Only 16 years old, Albert was disappointed, of course. He was also determined, though, not to let this early setback get in the way of his goal of playing professional baseball. He knew other chances would come.

Albert did not have much time for disappointment. A major change was about to take place in his family's life. Several members of the Pujols family had moved from Santo Domingo to the United States, to search for jobs and the chance for a better life. After hearing from them about the possibilities that existed in the United States, Albert's grandmother America decided that the time had come for the rest of the family to move there as well. The Pujolses would be heading to New York City.

The move would be a big change for Albert. He had never before left the Dominican Republic, and he spoke only Spanish. He would be leaving behind his home and friends to move to a new land with new possibilities. Would Albert be able to make the transition from the world he grew up in to the unknown world of New York City? How would the move affect his dreams of playing professional baseball?

A New Life

Albert Pujols and his family left the Dominican Republic in the summer of 1996, joining other members of his family in New York City. It is easy to imagine the reaction of the Pujols family, coming from Santo Domingo, upon seeing the city for the first time. Loud, crowded, and teeming with people of all different nationalities and races, New York must have seemed somewhat frightening and intimidating. Still, the United States offered the Pujols family new opportunities. As Albert later said, quoted in Jeff Savage's *Albert Pujols*, "We come from a poor, poor country. When we came to the United States, it was like, 'Oh man, we're in heaven!'"

The family did not remain in New York City for long. The city was more expensive than the family had ever imagined. Also, Albert's grandmother, America, was concerned that New

York City was not a safe place to raise her grandson. Her worst fears were soon realized.

One day, when Albert was going to the grocery store to pick up some items for his grandmother, he witnessed a man being shot to death just a few feet from where he was standing. When he returned home and told America what he had seen, she knew what she had to do: The family would have to find a safer place to live.

The Pujolses decided to move to the small city of Independence, Missouri, best known as the hometown of U.S. president

☆ ☆ ☆ ☆ ☆ ☆

DOMINICAN IMMIGRATION

Although Dominicans have been coming to the United States since the 1880s, it has only been since the 1960s that they have come in large numbers, mainly because of political and economic turmoil in their country. Immigration has continued until today, with nearly half of all Dominican immigrants in the United States arriving since the 1990s.

The majority of Dominican immigrants have settled in cities on the East Coast of the United States. Cities that are home to large numbers of Dominicans include New York City; Patterson, Passaic, and Perth Amboy, New Jersey; Lawrence and Boston, Massachusetts; Providence, Rhode Island; Philadelphia, Pennsylvania; and Baltimore, Maryland. Dominican Americans make up one of the largest Hispanic groups in the United States, behind Mexican Americans and Puerto Ricans.

Dominican Americans consider themselves to be of mixed race: a combination of European, African, and Amerindian ancestry. Almost 90 percent of Dominican Americans are Roman Catholic. Dominican food features white rice, beans, yucca,

Harry S. Truman. On the surface, it seems an odd choice. Why would a Spanish-speaking family from the Dominican Republic move to a town in the American Midwest?

Several factors went into the decision. The Pujols family had heard that Independence was already home to a small enclave of 2,000 Dominicans. They also felt that the small-town values of Independence would mesh nicely with their own family's values. The move turned out to be the right one, for Albert and the rest of his family.

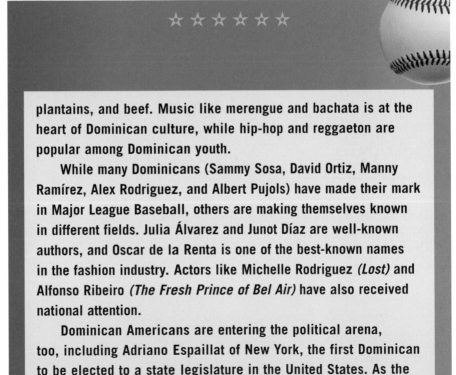

★ ★ ★ ★ ★

plantains, and beef. Music like merengue and bachata is at the heart of Dominican culture, while hip-hop and reggaeton are popular among Dominican youth.

While many Dominicans (Sammy Sosa, David Ortiz, Manny Ramírez, Alex Rodriguez, and Albert Pujols) have made their mark in Major League Baseball, others are making themselves known in different fields. Julia Álvarez and Junot Díaz are well-known authors, and Oscar de la Renta is one of the best-known names in the fashion industry. Actors like Michelle Rodriguez *(Lost)* and Alfonso Ribeiro *(The Fresh Prince of Bel Air)* have also received national attention.

Dominican Americans are entering the political arena, too, including Adriano Espaillat of New York, the first Dominican to be elected to a state legislature in the United States. As the next generation of Dominican Americans comes of age, they, too, will make their own contributions to American culture, enriching and enlarging it, just like every other group of immigrants.

When the family arrived in Independence, they settled into a small house that must have seemed like a mansion compared with their living situation in Santo Domingo. Many of Albert's aunts and uncles quickly found jobs as school-bus drivers. And Albert immediately took the opportunity to attend his first major-league game, watching the Kansas City Royals host the California Angels.

Albert enrolled at Fort Osage High School, where he was listed as a sophomore. Although he was a year older than his classmates, his lack of English held him back. To help, he was assigned a tutor, Portia Stanke, who worked with him every day for the two-and-a-half years he attended Fort Osage.

"It was tough the first year," Albert said, quoted in Jeff Savage's *Albert Pujols*. "I was shy. I knew that I needed English to communicate. So I worked hard at it, like baseball." Albert knew that his success in school and as a baseball player depended on his ability to learn English. Although he was frustrated at times by the difficulties of learning the language, he worked hard, and his English gradually improved.

Baseball, though, dominated nearly every waking moment of Albert's life. One of his first extracurricular activities at Fort Osage was joining the school's baseball team. His cousin, Wilfredo, introduced Albert to the coach, Dave Fry, who remembered the meeting well.

As quoted in *Albert the Great* by Rob Rains, Fry said of the meeting, "He was tall and good-looking, with big shoulders and a tiny waist. I told him, 'If you want to play, we're going to have a tryout session in February.' I didn't think about him anymore."

When February came around, Albert gave Fry every reason to think about him. It was then that Fry became one of the first to realize young Albert's potential as a batter—just from hearing him hit the ball. "I heard this 'whack, whack, whack.'" Fry remembered, quoted in *Albert the Great*. "I thought, 'What in the world?' I went and took a look, and Albert was in the cage, lining some shots. 'Gee, boy, what have we got here?' I said. He was a man among boys."

At times, though, Albert's limited English skills made communication between coach and player difficult. "Any teaching, any communication, most of the time I would act it out or show him what I was trying to get across," Fry said, quoted in *Albert the Great*. "He would keep me up all night taking ground balls, but his forte was hitting."

Fry told *Sports Illustrated*, "Language was Albert's biggest barrier. He had trouble understanding when you explained rules and regulations to him. But he loved baseball. You could get anything about baseball through to him, how to move his hands when he hit, where to set his feet when he was fielding."

Indeed, there was little at this point for Fry to teach Albert about his game. He did, though, make one suggestion as to where to put his hands when he was taking his stance, a stance perhaps copied from his boyhood idol Julio Franco. "He held the bat up high and I said to him, 'You might find it helpful to lower your hands a bit.' That was it. Everything was natural for him."

As with almost everyone else who has watched Pujols play over the years, Fry was most impressed with the teenager's hitting ability. "You only had to see Albert swing the bat once or twice to notice that he had some pretty good power," Fry said, quoted in *Albert the Great*. "I never saw a kid swing so hard on every pitch. Not just once in a while, but every pitch. At our school, we have a short left-field porch, and he constantly bombarded that house behind our fence."

Albert played shortstop in high school, but his main role was as a hitter. In his first season, he hit .471 with 11 home runs and 32 RBIs, leading Fort Osage to the Missouri Class 4A state championship in 1997.

His English tutor, Portia Stanke, remembers the pride that Albert felt playing on the Fort Osage varsity team. She recalled, quoted in *Albert the Great,* "Albert was always so proud to wear his baseball uniform to class the day he had a game. But when he came back the next day, he never bragged about what he [had accomplished in the game]. You only knew if you asked him."

In just his first year as a player, Albert had established himself as the hardest worker—and hitter—on the team. The following season, 1998, opposing coaches and pitchers knew the player they were facing. During this season, Albert walked 55 times in only 88 plate appearances. This early demonstration of his ability to select pitches showed his discipline as a batter, despite his frustration at not being pitched anything he could hit. "They would let him bat one time and then walk him. Albert got pretty fed up with that. But if I was the opponent, I would have done it, too," Fry said, quoted in *Albert the Great.*

Despite this, he still managed to hit eight home runs in those 33 non-walk at-bats, including one mammoth homer that people who witnessed it remember to this day.

That ball was hit with such force that it landed on top of a 25-foot-tall (7.6-meter-tall) air-conditioning unit that was on top of a building nearly 40 feet (12 meters) beyond the left-field fence. It is estimated that the ball had to have traveled at least 450 feet (137 meters). "The ball just traveled and traveled and traveled," Fry remembered, quoted in *Albert the Great.* "I didn't think it would ever come down."

Albert was disappointed with his failure to be selected to the Kansas City All-Metro first team either year. As a junior, though, he was selected as the second-team shortstop. The main reason he did not make the first team? Albert had made more than 20 errors at shortstop, most of them throwing errors.

Fry had a theory about why Albert made so many errors, as quoted in *Albert the Great.* "Dominican players never actually set their feet. They're constantly throwing sidearm or underhanded. We were trying to get Albert to field the ball, go from

Albert Pujols got caught up on the left-field wall after trying to catch a home run hit by Jeff Conine of the Orioles during a game in June 2003. In his first few years in the major leagues, Pujols played first base, third base, left field, and right field. When he was in high school, he played shortstop. Baseball scouts knew that shortstop was not a natural position for Pujols, but they also had trouble figuring out where he should play in the field.

the ground to the gut, point the shoulder and step and throw. That's a lot of things to say." In other words, Albert's still-shaky command of the English language made it difficult for his coach to give him the instructions he needed.

Still, despite his fielding problems, Albert was beginning to catch the notice of baseball scouts. They knew that shortstop was not a natural position for him, but they had a hard time imagining what position he should play. And, because he was still only a junior in high school, despite being 18 years old, he was ineligible for the baseball draft.

Albert first came to the attention of the St. Louis Cardinals in the summer between his junior and senior years in high school. Playing in the Area Code Games, he was spotted by Mike Roberts, a cross-checker scout for the Cardinals. (A cross-checker is a veteran scout who looks at prospects recommended by area scouts.) Roberts's brother-in-law, Dave Karaff, was the area scout for the team and had told him about the young hitting prodigy.

"The first thing you noticed about him was his strength," Roberts said, quoted in *Albert the Great*. "He was not as big physically as he is now, but you could tell that he could hit." Roberts and other scouts, however, did not necessarily consider Pujols a top prospect—there were still too many questions about where he could play in the field.

Roberts is quoted in *Albert the Great* as saying, "I know one guy who saw him and the only thing he wrote down on his report was 4.7, the time he ran going to first base. He was not the kind of player that was going to blow you away when you first saw him. I just saw size and strength."

Knowing of Albert's goal of playing professional baseball, some scouts suggested to him that he would have a better chance of being drafted if he graduated high school early and entered a junior college. If he continued to play high school ball, teams would continue to pitch around him as they had during his junior year, and scouts would never be able to get a true reading of his skills. Certain that this was the path that would lead him to the majors, Pujols settled on an aggressive courseload for the fall semester of his senior year, allowing him to graduate in January 1999.

One of the few breaks he took from studying that fall was to play in the all-star game for high school students in the Kansas City area. There, his playing caught the eye of Marty Kilgore, the coach at nearby Maple Woods Community College, a junior college. Kilgore, who thought that watching Pujols was like watching a man playing with boys, persuaded Pujols to attend Maple Woods.

MEETING DEIDRE

Although Albert's life was devoted to baseball, he still had some time for normal teenage activities. He hung out with his friends on weekends and enjoyed going to malls and clubs. One night, while still a senior, Albert went out to Cashmere, a Latin dance club in Kansas City. There, he met Deidre Corona, a pretty 21-year-old.

The couple spent the evening dancing and getting to know each other, even though Deidre spoke no Spanish and Albert still spoke little English. Albert, who was already falling in love with Deidre, lied and told her that he was also 21, the minimum age a person could be to enter the club. Gathering up all his nerve, he asked Deidre for her phone number, which she readily gave him. Within a matter of days, he called and asked her out on a date.

She said yes, and on that first date Albert told her that he had a confession to make, that he had lied about his age the night they met at the club. Deidre, thinking that he must be older, asked him if he was 22 or even 23. Imagine her surprise when he told her he was only 18. "You're barely legal!" she exclaimed.

It turned out, though, that Deidre had a confession of her own to make. Deidre, who had grown up in the Kansas City area, had been to college and was working as a secretary. But that was not the confession. Deidre told Albert that she was a single mother of an eight-week-old girl.

The news did not change Albert's interest in Deidre, and the couple continued to spend time together. One week later, Deidre told Albert that she had one more piece of news that she had not told him about her daughter. It was something she knew she had to tell, but Deidre was concerned that the news could end their rapidly blossoming romance.

4

Moving Up

The news that Deidre Corona had to tell Albert Pujols was that her daughter, Isabella, had been born with Down syndrome. Deidre explained that the condition caused learning problems and physical challenges. Concerned that Albert's less-than-perfect English skills might cause him to misunderstand what she was telling him, she gave him pamphlets written in Spanish about the condition.

Reading the pamphlets, Albert learned that Down syndrome is a genetic disorder named after John Langdon Down, the British doctor who first described it in 1866. Many children born with Down syndrome have common physical characteristics: a flatter face, upward-slanting eyes, and a somewhat larger tongue. Some may have small or misshapen ears, a large space between the big toe and the second toe, and a crease that goes

across the palms of their hands. They usually have some developmental disability, which can cause difficulty in learning.

Babies with Down syndrome tend to develop later and more slowly than other babies do. They may start walking later than other babies. About half of the children with Down syndrome are born with heart defects (as was Isabella), but those problems can usually be corrected with surgery (as was Isabella's). Some babies may also have problems in their stomachs or have a blockage in their intestines that prevents them from digesting food properly.

Children with Down syndrome are also more likely to get infections that affect their lungs and breathing. Those infections often tend to last longer than usual. They may have eye or ear problems or digestion problems such as constipation. Some may develop leukemia. But, as Albert read, each person with Down syndrome is different and may have one, several, or all of these problems.

The syndrome is caused by a genetic defect. Most people have 23 pairs of chromosomes, the threadlike substances within each cell that carry genes, for a total of 46 chromosomes. Babies born with Down syndrome have three copies of Chromosome 21, instead of two copies. It is this extra genetic material that causes problems with the way the babies' bodies develop. About one out of every 800 babies is born with Down syndrome. There is no cure.

In an interview with KSDK television in St. Louis, Deidre said that, even before receiving the diagnosis from her doctor, God had told her that her daughter would be a special-needs baby. "I heard Him; I mean, He told me she had Down syndrome. I was very emotional. I was at one point crying hysterically, but when they wheeled her in and she had her little cap and she was wrapped up, I mean, I just saw, I've never seen such a moment of innocence."

Isabella, though, was Deidre's child and *her* responsibility. It is easy to imagine Deidre's feelings as she watched

Albert read the pamphlets about Down syndrome. Raising a child with Down syndrome is a challenge for any parent. It would have been very easy for Albert to just walk away from the relationship. Why would an 18-year-old with dreams of playing professional baseball want to take on that kind of challenge?

Albert, though, was not just any teenager. Demonstrating a strength and maturity well beyond his years, he had no intention of ending his relationship with Deidre because of her daughter's condition. Instead, as Deidre said, quoted in Jeff Savage's *Albert Pujols*, after getting the information, "he was almost in tears. His heart was so tender about it." When Albert finally met Isabella, he said that he immediately saw himself as her father.

The couple stayed together after Albert graduated early from high school, and Albert stayed home and took care of Isabella while Deidre was at work. Albert and Deidre learned that they had much in common despite their different backgrounds. She had grown up in a stable family, very different from Albert's childhood. Yet, they still wanted the same things.

As Deidre said, quoted in *Albert the Great*, "My parents were together and supported me in everything. I know what family values are. Albert grew up in the Dominican Republic with no mom, his dad going off for long periods of time to work, so his grandma and his grandpa were the ones there for him. There was always movement in Albert's life, not the secure home that I think a child needs. I'm really amazed that Albert came out with really strong family values."

Deidre has called Albert her earthly savior, the man who helped her break away from a fast crowd. She said in her interview with KDSK, "I really think I could have fallen back into that pattern had it not been for him because he didn't drink, he didn't smoke, he wasn't even old enough to be [in those places]. All he did was play ball and go to school."

MAPLE WOODS COMMUNITY COLLEGE

At the same time that his relationship with Deidre was deepening, Albert entered Maple Woods Community College. On his first day of practice, he met Landon Brandes, a sophomore and the team's leading hitter. Brandes remembered that first practice in *Albert the Great*.

"Everyone was using metal bats. Albert stepped in with a wood bat. I was hitting some out of the park before that, and I felt pretty good." Pujols then hit the ball at least 50 feet (15 meters) farther than any of the balls that Brandes had hit. "Are you kidding me?" Brandes thought. "This kid is right out of high school, and he's out-blasting me?"

Pujols made a great impression in the season's first game. He hit a grand slam off of Mark Buehrle, a future all-star with the Chicago White Sox, and still playing at shortstop, turned an unassisted triple play. That debut was just the start of a huge season for Pujols, who finished with a .461 average, along with 22 home runs and 80 RBIs.

At Maple Woods, just as at Fort Osage High School, he hit a home run that people still talk about. Playing against Highland Community College in Kansas, Pujols hit the ball so well that it flew out of the park, across the street, and directly into a tree!

In another game, Pujols hit a ball into a 30-mile-per-hour (48-kilometer-per-hour) wind and was upset that he only managed to get a triple out of it. Coach Marty Kilgore said, quoted in *Albert the Great*, "He was pretty mad about it. He didn't think the wind should have mattered."

Kilgore went on, discussing what it was like to coach Pujols at this stage of his life. "He had baseball instincts that just couldn't be taught. The way he would run the bases, going from second to third when a third baseman came up throwing across . . . just knowing how much to get off so they wouldn't throw behind him . . . just the little things you can't teach that made him a special player. He was the best athlete I've ever seen with the baseball skills and power."

Mark Buehrle, playing here in 2002 against the Minnesota Twins, is an all-star pitcher for the Chicago White Sox. Buehrle was the opposing pitcher in Pujols's first game at Maple Woods Community College, and Pujols had a great start—he hit a grand slam off Buehrle.

Propelled by Pujols's hitting, the Centaurs went to the regional National Junior College Athletic Association (NJCAA) championship but fell just one game short of making the trip to the national World Series. By this point of the season, Pujols's hitting abilities had become widely known. In one game against Seminole, Oklahoma, the pitchers tried to keep Pujols and Brandes from having a chance to get a hit by hitting them with a pitch each time they came to bat.

"Every time they hit Albert, he would just stand there, look at them, and stare them down," Kilgore remembered, quoted in *Albert the Great.* "Nothing scares him."

Pujols's play was once again catching the attention of baseball scouts. Dave Karaff, the scout for the St. Louis Cardinals who had noticed him back at Fort Osage High School, had a renewed interest in Pujols after watching him play college ball. "He stood out for me," Karaff said, quoted in *Albert the Great.* "He hit more long home runs. You could see the power and the strength."

Given Pujols's obvious talent, though, the Cardinals were not the only team keeping an eye on him. The area scout for the Tampa Bay Devil Rays was so impressed with Pujols that he had him flown to Tampa for a private workout just before the June draft. The workout did not go well. Maybe the people in charge did not like him, maybe Pujols had a bad day. Whatever the reason, the Devil Rays showed no further interest.

As any baseball scout knows, success in scouting is not an exact science. So much of it is a matter of luck and timing— being at the right place at the right time to see a player at his best. Karaff experienced this when he brought a cross-checker to watch Pujols play, quoted in *Albert the Great.*

"I had never seen Albert strike out on a fastball, and the day I brought the regional cross-checker in to see him, he struck out twice on fastballs and in another at-bat fell down running over first base. Luckily for me, the scout came back the next day, too, and saw him hit one out of sight."

DRAFT DAY

Mike Roberts and Dave Karaff both believed strongly enough in Pujols's talent and long-term potential as a baseball player that they knew he was worth selecting in the 1999 draft. Both scouts, longtime professionals, expected him to be selected between the sixth and the tenth rounds. After the tenth round of the draft had been completed and Pujols still had not been selected, Roberts, who was sitting in the Cardinals' draft room, began to plead even harder with his bosses to select Pujols.

While this drama was unfolding, another team was considering a move for Pujols. Ernie Jacobs, a Boston Red Sox scout, was urging his bosses to draft Pujols as well. "I won't say that I thought he'd be the player that he has become," Jacobs told the *Boston Globe*, "but I liked him in the third or fourth round. That's where I liked him."

The problem for the Red Sox, as well as for the Cardinals, was that not everyone in the two organizations agreed with the scouts' reports. "First of all," Jacobs said, "his body wasn't great back then. . . . And his swing was a little long.

"But he had big-time power, and you can't walk away from that kind of power. You do your homework, you study his aptitude, you figure you can fine-tune his swing and get his body better. His hands were very good for his size, and he had a good arm, playing shortstop."

At the start of the tenth round of the draft, at the same time that Roberts was urging the Cardinals to pick up Pujols, Jacobs received a phone call. "They called and told me they were going to draft Albert for me," Jacobs said. "But there were a couple of stipulations. First of all, can he play third base for Lowell [a Boston farm team]? I told them, 'Sure he can.' Then they said, 'He's got to be a quick sign.' I said, 'We may have a little issue.' I remember the kid saying he wanted to sign for $100,000, $150,000. I had a feeling that it wasn't going to take that, but it might drag out all summer."

Jacobs tried to reach Pujols by phone, but Deidre answered, saying that Albert was not home. She called Jacobs back an hour and a half later, saying that she still had not been able to reach him. By then it was too late. "They told me that they were going to pass if he wasn't a quick sign," Jacobs said. "The Cardinals took him three rounds later, and the rest is history."

While the Red Sox were making their move, Roberts was begging his bosses not to lose Pujols. He argued that the other Cardinal scouts had not had enough chances to see him play, and, knowing that he would not be able to play shortstop in the majors, they had not given him a fair evaluation.

"He moved OK, and he had a good enough arm that I thought he could maybe play third base," Roberts said, quoted in *Albert the Great.* "I knew for sure he ought to be able to play first. What I saw I liked, but I knew what was going to carry him was his bat. I thought, if he hit, we could find a position for him to play."

Karaff, too, was convinced that Pujols was draft-worthy. "I had some reservations about how well he was going to hit. I knew he would hit some home runs, and I didn't think he would strike out a lot, so I thought he was a guy worth taking a chance on."

Finally, in the thirteenth round, the Cardinals listened to Roberts and selected Pujols. "We were lucky," Roberts said. "I think we got him because I happened to be there and had a chance to talk about him in the room. The area scout who had sent in all the reports wasn't there, but because we had somebody who liked him there at the end, we were able to take him."

Although Pujols was not disappointed that he had been selected by the Cardinals, he was upset that he had not been picked until the thirteenth round. That meant that 400 players had been chosen by all the major-league teams before he had been selected. Pujols was so hurt and upset that he briefly considered giving up baseball forever.

"It did bother me, I won't lie. I was disappointed," Pujols said years later, quoted in *Albert the Great.* "I thought maybe I should quit baseball." Maybe, he thought, he would go into engineering or medicine.

After thinking it over, Pujols realized that he could not give up on his dream of playing professional baseball. His pride, however, would not allow him to accept the Cardinals' initial contract and $10,000 signing bonus. Instead, he agreed to play in Hays, Kansas, for the collegiate Jayhawk summer league. To save on expenses, he moved in with his new coach, Frank Leo, and Leo's wife, Barb. To pursue his life's goal, he would have to live apart from Deidre and Isabella for the summer.

Pujols had a good season, leading his team in home runs and batting average as well as impressing Leo with his talents as a player and his maturity off the field. He tried to be prepared for every situation he might encounter on the field, and he spent his evenings getting advice from his coaches rather than going out with friends.

"He was so aware of everything," Leo said, quoted in *Albert the Great*. "How to hit certain kinds of pitchers, how to run the bases, how to play every situation. He came to us with a purpose in mind. He had a goal, and he wasn't going to be distracted from it."

It was Deidre's mother, Linda Corona, who urged Pujols to get over his disappointment, swallow his pride, and sign with the Cardinals at the end of the summer season. Pujols took her advice. "I decided I didn't care too much about where I got drafted," he said, quoted in *Albert the Great*. "I knew if I was good enough, I would make it to the big leagues in three or four years."

Pujols signed a $65,000 package with the Cardinals, including a signing bonus as well as money to pay his college expenses. "He was such a great kid; I really liked him," Karaff recalled fondly. "I knew he wanted to play, and we finally got it done."

Just three years after leaving the Dominican Republic with his family, Pujols's dream had become a reality. He was a professional baseball player. Now, he would have to prove himself all over again, against the best baseball players in the country. He would have to prove himself worthy of playing in the big leagues.

PLAYING IN THE MINORS

Because he had signed with the Cardinals so late in the season, Pujols was not able to join a regular minor-league team in 1999. Instead, he flew to Jupiter, Florida, where he joined the Cardinals' Instructional League team for further training. He quickly made his presence felt.

On his very first swing at Roger Dean Stadium, Pujols smashed a line drive that flew straight over the left-field wall and bounced off the offices of the Montreal Expos, far outside the outfield wall. (The Expos and Cardinals shared the training complex.) Later that day, he repeated the feat. Mike Jorgensen, the Cardinals' director of player management, was in the stands that day and remembered how impressed he was by Pujols's performance.

"In spring training you see the big boys popping the ball up there, but usually during the Instructional League you hardly see anyone hit it over the fence," Jorgensen said, quoted in *Albert the Great.* He was so impressed watching Pujols play over the next few days that he asked the scouts why Pujols had not been drafted until the thirteenth round.

"I was told some scouts thought he was heavy and didn't move that well, but everybody had to see the bat. It stood out that much. A lot of [other teams] missed the boat, but [we] were lucky to get him." The Cardinals were beginning to realize what they had gotten with Pujols. He hit .323 in the Instructional League and began to learn a new position—third base. The Cardinals already had a young and powerful third baseman named Fernando Tatis, but the team's management figured that Pujols would not be ready for the big leagues until Tatis was in his late 20s.

That winter, Pujols returned home, and he and Deidre were married on New Year's Day, January 1, 2000. (Deidre jokes that she chose the date so that there would be no way Albert could ever forget their anniversary!) After the wedding, Albert, Deidre, and Isabella were rarely separated. In fact, when

Pujols was assigned to the Peoria Chiefs of the Class A Midwest League at the start of the 2000 season, Deidre and Isabella moved there with him.

★ ★ ★ ★ ★ ☆

MINOR-LEAGUE BASEBALL

The minor leagues are North American professional baseball leagues that compete at a level beneath that of Major League Baseball. All of the leagues are considered independent businesses, but the best-known ones are members of Minor League Baseball, an umbrella organization for leagues that have agreements to operate as affiliates of Major League Baseball.

Each league that is part of Minor League Baseball has teams that are directly affiliated with (and occasionally named after) one major-league team. For example, the Iowa Cubs have been affiliated with and named after the Chicago Cubs since 1981, but the Columbus Clippers changed their affiliation for the 2007 season from the New York Yankees to the Washington Nationals. A small number of minor-league teams are directly owned by their major-league "parent."

The purpose of this system is to develop players who will be available to play in the major leagues on demand. Today, 20 minor baseball leagues operate with 246 clubs in towns big and small across the United States and Canada.

Minor-league baseball also goes by the nickname "the farm system" because of a joke told by major-league players in the 1930s, when St. Louis Cardinals general manager Branch Rickey formalized the minor-league system. Back then, it was said that they were "growing players down on the farm like corn." In other words, at the minor-league level, the players are "grown" until they're "ripe enough" to be harvested and brought up to the major leagues.

At Peoria, the team manager was Tom Lawless, a former infielder for the Cardinals; he immediately recognized that Pujols stood out from most of the other players on his team and in the league. Lawless said, quoted in *Albert the Great*:

> We knew he needed to work on defense, but you could tell he was an outstanding hitter. His mechanics were so good that he was taking the pitch from the middle of the plate out and hitting it to right-center and right field. That is usually a skill you have to teach young hitters; they normally try to pull everything.
>
> As the pitchers began to scout him, they started to work him inside, and he was still trying to hit the pitch the other way. We had to teach him to get the barrel of the bat through the zone quicker so he could pull that pitch to left field. It didn't take him long to figure it out.

While Pujols settled into his first season in the minors, the family struggled to make ends meet. The well-publicized high paychecks of major-league players do not exist in the minors, and the Pujols family had to survive on a paycheck of just $252 every two weeks. Living in a small, poorly furnished apartment, Deidre did whatever she could to help the family.

As she recalled in her interview with KDSK television, "I did whatever it took. I never just sat around hoping for the money angel to drop out of the sky. I mean I worked. I sold Mary Kay [cosmetics] to be with Albert. In order to work it from that angle, I had to find places in Peoria that could assist Bella with her special needs."

No matter how well he was playing, Pujols was still not satisfied with his performance. Not happy with his hitting, even though he was batting over .300, he worked hard with the batting coach. Lawless spent hours working with him on playing third base. As always, Pujols was a good student, and his hard work paid off. Playing as the team's everyday third baseman, he was named the league's top defensive player with the best infield arm.

Although the Chiefs were not a great team across the board, the heart of their batting order was strong, with Pujols joined by future big-league players Chris Duncan and Ben Johnson. The 2000 season of the Midwest League was dominated by pitching (seven no-hitters were thrown). Still, Pujols finished second in the league with a .324 batting average, and 32 doubles, 17 home runs, and 84 RBIs. He also showed his continued discipline at the plate, striking out only 37 times in 395 at-bats.

Even though Pujols enjoyed playing in the Midwest League, he had his eyes on the major leagues. Peoria was only a few hours north of St. Louis, so whenever he had the opportunity, Pujols traveled down to Busch Stadium to watch the Cardinals play and to dream of the day that he, too, would be down there on the field.

Everybody who watched Pujols play for the Chiefs knew that it was only a matter of time before he was promoted. In August 2000, Pujols was sent to the Cardinals' high Class A team, the Cannons in Potomac, Virginia. Just a few days before the promotion was announced, Pujols had smashed a home run that sailed high over the left-field fence and landed on top of the team's dressing room. His coach, Tom Lawless, knew he was ready to make the move.

"As well as he could hit going the opposite way, as soon as he learned to hit the inside pitch to left field, I knew he was on his way," Lawless said, quoted in *Albert the Great.* "He has such strong hands, and his hand-eye coordination is so good, that was the secret to his success." Pujols was voted Midwest League MVP and shared honors with Austin Kearns, a future Cincinnati Reds player, as the league's two best prospects.

Just months after settling in Peoria, Pujols was playing for the Potomac Cannons for the last month of the 2000 season. Sitting in the stands during Pujols's first game with the

Albert Pujols ended up playing for three minor-league teams in 2000. Here, he is at bat for the Potomac Cannons in Virginia. He played most of the year for Peoria in the Class A Midwest League before spending a month with the Cannons in a high Class A league. Then, he joined the Memphis Redbirds for their play-off run in the Class AAA Pacific Coast League.

Cannons was Walt Jocketty, the St. Louis Cardinals' general manager.

"He came to bat with runners in scoring position," Jocketty remembered, quoted in *Albert the Great.* "I think he was behind in the count 1-2, and [he hit] the next pitch [for a] base hit up the middle for an RBI. Same thing with his next at-bat, in an almost identical situation. I said, 'Man, this guy gets off the plane, and he already is an RBI machine.'"

Pujols played just 22 games with the Cannons before the season ended. He hit .284 with two home runs and 10 RBIs, and he again demonstrated his discipline at the plate by striking out only eight times in 81 at-bats.

Although the regular season was over, Pujols continued to play and move up the minor-league ladder. Outfielder Ernie Young had left the Cardinals' Class AAA club in Memphis to become part of the U.S. Olympic Team. Memphis manager Gaylen Pitts needed a right-handed batter that he could use off the bench for the Pacific Coast League play-offs. Pitts contacted Mike Jorgensen, the Cardinals' director of player management, for help.

"We knew for about three weeks Memphis was going to be playing Albuquerque [in the play-offs], and they had three left-handed starters," Jorgensen said, quoted in *Albert the Great.* "I was looking at the list of free agents and guys who had been released, and Pitts finally said to me one day, 'What about Pujols?'"

Jorgensen pointed out to Pitts that Pujols had only one year of professional baseball experience, all on the Class A level, but Pitts was not to be deterred. He suggested to Jorgensen that Pujols be promoted to Memphis early to give him a few days to prepare for playing Class AAA ball. Then, Pitts said, he would have a chance to evaluate whether Pujols was ready to play at that level before the play-off rosters were set. Jorgensen agreed, and Pujols was soon playing for his third team in just one year.

Although Jorgensen was concerned about the move, he thought it would be a good experience for Pujols. Jorgensen was worried about Pujols moving up too quickly, but he knew that Pujols was a terrific hitter, coming off a great season. It was time to give him an opportunity to prove himself.

And prove himself he did. He played so well that he was added to the play-off roster as a left fielder, even though he had played third base all season. Pujols demonstrated that he was more than ready to play at the Class AAA level, hitting .302 in 11 postseason games. Not only that, he hit a game- and pennant-winning home run in the thirteenth inning against Salt Lake City to give Memphis the Pacific Coast League championship. Not surprisingly, Pujols was named the play-off MVP.

Pujols's season still was not over. After the Pacific Coast League championships, he went to Scottsdale, Arizona, to play in the Arizona Fall League as one of the game's best prospects. In 27 games, he hit .323 with 4 home runs and 21 RBIs, good enough to be voted by the league's managers and coaches as the best third-base prospect in the league. He was one of only three players to be named on every ballot.

Pujols had had a remarkable first season in the minors, but now that it was over, he still had a wife and a daughter to support. To save money, the family moved in with Deidre's parents in Kansas City, and Pujols got a job working at the Meadowbrook Country Club. There, he set up rooms for par- ties and other catering functions.

The money would come in extra-handy in January, when Deidre gave birth to the couple's first child, a son named Albert, Jr., nicknamed A.J.

When Pujols was not working at the country club or spending time with his growing family, he was working hard to hone his baseball skills. He even spent two hours a day lifting weights. "Lifting, lifting, lifting," said Pujols, quoted in Jeff Savage's *Albert Pujols.* "I worked hard to get stronger."

The Cardinals had plans for Pujols to skip the Class AA level and start the 2001 season at Class AAA Memphis, a team just one level beneath the major leagues. That spring, Pujols reported to his first big-league training camp, prepared to spend the season playing for Memphis. Like so much else in his short career, however, events would overtake the best-laid plans.

In the Big Leagues

When spring training began in 2001, the plan was that Albert Pujols, still just 21 years old, would spend the year playing for the Memphis Redbirds, honing his skills until he was deemed ready to play in the majors. For many Cardinals executives, who had only heard reports of his minor-league triumphs, spring-training camp would be their first opportunity to see him play.

Arriving at camp, Pujols was assigned uniform No. 68. The number, a relatively high one, indicated that the Cardinals did not expect him to be playing in the majors—at least not immediately. Pujols's roommate was Landon Brandes, his old friend and teammate from Maple Woods Community College. Brandes had been drafted by St. Louis in 2000. At night, the two old friends would talk about how they thought training was going and speculate on their chances of making it to the majors.

"He'd say, 'Tomorrow I'm going to go out and get a couple of hits,'" Brandes said, quoted in *Albert the Great*. "He knew what kind of game plan he would have already. It wasn't him being cocky. It was just him saying, 'This is my job, to get a couple of hits and a couple of RBIs.'"

The question of which position he would play, however, remained. The Cardinals' previous third baseman, Fernando Tatis, had been traded to the Montreal Expos over the winter. The Cardinals thought that veterans Craig Paquette and Plácido Polanco would hold the position until Pujols was ready to join the majors. Such a move, though, was thought to be at least a year away.

Pujols had other plans and no intention of being sent back to Memphis. His goal was to play so well that Tony La Russa, the Cardinals' manager, would *have* to put him on the roster. He had his first chance to make an impression when live batting practice began in late February at the Cardinals' training camp in Jupiter, Florida. Although pitching coach Dave Duncan was carefully monitoring his pitchers, he could not help but notice Pujols.

"He was taking really professional at-bats," Duncan said, quoted in *Albert the Great*. "You could tell he was determined to compete. . . . He wasn't going to do something in the cage in February that was going to create a bad habit or give a bad impression."

He was, in fact, making a great impression. La Russa noticed him—he speculated on Pujols's talent and how long it would take him to make the big leagues. Still, there was no obvious position in which to place him on the roster. The everyday lineup seemed set with Mark McGwire, Fernando Viña, Edgar Rentería, and Craig Paquette in the infield, Ray Lankford, Jim Edmonds, and J.D. Drew in the outfield, and several strong bench players, including John Mabry and Bobby Bonilla. Fate, though, was determined to give Pujols a helping hand.

McGwire and Bonilla were both injured, giving La Russa an opportunity to play Pujols in spring-training games. Pujols knew that this could be his big break, and he seized the opportunity.

La Russa played Pujols in the outfield and at first base, in addition to third base. Although his hitting got him noticed, several fielding plays caught La Russa's attention as well, including a diving catch in the outfield with the bases loaded that robbed Mike Piazza of the New York Mets of a hit. Some Cardinals coaches thought that La Russa was working Pujols extra hard, hoping he would give the manager a reason to send him back to the minors. But no reason came. Pujols passed every challenge that La Russa could throw at him.

"It was impossible to get him to perform poorly, and I pushed him," La Russa said, quoted in *Albert the Great*. "Dave Duncan accused me of trying to find a place where he couldn't play, but Albert refused to cooperate. I kept using him against the toughest pitchers, and he kept hitting."

As spring training progressed, the club began to trim its roster, sending players down to the minors. Each week, Pujols made the cut, avoiding being sent to Memphis.

At the time, the Cardinals shared their spring-training complex with the Montreal Expos and played them frequently. La Russa took the opportunity to ask the Expos' manager, Felipe Alou, what he thought about Pujols.

"I told him I liked him a lot," Alou said, quoted in *Albert the Great*. "It seemed like everything he hit that spring was hard. As spring training came to a close, Tony told me he was thinking about carrying the kid on the roster, even though he lacked experience. . . . He's truly what I would call a phenom with a bat. One year out of Class A, and he was hitting like that."

Week after week, Pujols impressed one and all with his powerful hitting. One week before the regular season was

In this portrait taken during spring training in 2001, Albert Pujols is wearing a No. 68 Cardinals uniform. He was given such a high number because the Cardinals did not expect Pujols to stay at the major-league level for the regular season. He did make the Cardinals' roster, however, and his number was switched to 5.

to begin, Pujols was in the batter's box again. McGwire, the Cardinals' first baseman, was sitting in the dugout, talking with La Russa. "What do you think? We going to take him?" McGwire asked the manager. "A lot of us think he should make the club." As if to punctuate the question, Pujols smashed the next pitch over the wall for another home run. As the ball cleared the scoreboard, McGwire prodded La Russa with his elbow, saying, as quoted in *Albert the Great*, "Did you see that? How are you not going to take him?"

It was not just his playing that impressed La Russa, the other coaches, and his teammates. Pujols also stood out because of his drive, his determination to improve his game, and his sheer love of baseball.

One day, for example, after Pujols had played in a long series of games, La Russa decided to give him the day off in the next game against the Florida Marlins. Imagine La Russa's surprise when, one hour before the game started, he saw Pujols on the field taking groundballs at shortstop. The driven Pujols grabbed at any opportunity to practice, to play the game, to get better. The next day, La Russa started him at shortstop, where he initiated a double play on the first ball hit to him.

Despite Pujols's obvious talent, drive and determination, La Russa was still reluctant to put him on the roster. He knew that with no permanent position open, Pujols would be, at best, a part-time player. If Pujols were sent to Memphis, he would be able to play every day, gaining valuable experience. In many ways, it would be in Pujols's own interest to be playing in Memphis. Once again, though, fate in the form of injury stepped in and changed Pujols's life.

THE BIG SHOW

During spring training, Pujols hit .349 and led the club with 34 total bases and only eight strikeouts in 62 at-bats. Despite these numbers, it looked as if he was headed to Memphis for the 2001 season. No position on the roster was available. Just days before the start of the regular season, however, Bobby Bonilla pulled a hamstring and was placed on the disabled list. Pujols was now on the team, having made the big leagues with only three games of regular-season experience above the Class A level.

Pujols was thrilled to get the opportunity, but he knew that it could end at any time. La Russa warned him that the move was only guaranteed through the team's opening series in Colorado. Another decision would be made as soon as Bonilla was healthy. Pujols did not care, though. He knew that he had been given his big chance and that he was not going to fail. With a new No. 5 jersey replacing his No. 68 jersey, he was ready to play.

OPENING DAY

For anyone who is not a professional baseball player, it is probably hard to imagine what is going through the mind of a player making his big-league debut. All the years of training, all the practice hitting, catching, and throwing, all the hopes and dreams, finally coming to fruition in front of a huge crowd of baseball fans. It must be an emotionally overwhelming experience.

Different players react in different ways. George Brett, for example, says he was not nervous at all. At least until he saw his name on the lineup card. Then, as he remembers it, as quoted in Josh Lewin's *You Never Forget Your First*, "I suddenly had to go to the bathroom real bad." Jim Thome found himself so overwhelmed by the experience that he cannot even remember whether his team won or lost. Lance Berkman recalls being so nervous at his first at-bat that he could barely stand up. For Torii Hunter, his first game in the big leagues was the first time he had ever been in a major-league stadium, making it the first major-league game he had ever seen live.

Manny Ramírez spoke for many players when he said, quoted in *You Never Forget Your First*, "Anyone that tells you they don't have butterflies that first day is lying to you. . . . I could feel the butterflies in my stomach every minute. On the way to the stadium, more butterflies. In the clubhouse, butterflies, and when I saw I'd be playing, I could hardly breathe, man." As Cal Ripken said, quoted in *You Never Forget Your First*, "Excitement just shoots through you when [the call-up] happens. You can't sleep the whole night. I know I didn't."

For Albert Pujols, though, his reaction seems to have been different. Once again showing a maturity and self-confidence far beyond his years, he seems not to have had a moment of nervousness or fear. Unlike many other players, he never seems to have had a second's doubt that he would make it into the big leagues or that, once there, he would succeed.

To Pujols, he was still just playing baseball, the same game he had always loved, the game that he had played on the streets of the Dominican Republic as a young kid. He knew in his heart that he belonged in the big leagues.

Still, it was a day that would stay in his memories, as he recalled in *You Never Forget Your First*:

> My family called me. They knew before I did! We were finishing spring training by playing two games up in Seattle. And I guess it was being reported back in St. Louis and Kansas City that I was going to make the team. So my phone rang in my hotel room around 7:00 A.M., woke me up, and it was my parents. They said, "Yeah, it's all over the news, you're going to open in the big leagues," but I told them, "Until I hear it from the manager, I won't get excited." Later, Tony La Russa made it official. Bobby Bonilla wasn't going to be able to play right away because he was hurt, and that's what opened up the spot for them to take me. I gave myself permission to be excited then.
>
> I'd had a really good spring, and there was a lot of talk about how well I was doing, so it wasn't a complete surprise, but wow, it was still unbelievable. There I was in Colorado

for Opening Day. It wasn't like, "Oh man, I'm in the big leagues," because I always thought I could achieve that. It was just very special to be there for the Opening Day ceremonies. I will always remember the F-16 planes that went overhead during the anthem. They came up overhead, and it was so loud and so inspiring. They didn't have that [at] Opening Day in Peoria the year before, I can tell you that!

I'll remember my first hit always—up the middle, off Mike Hampton, and I still have the ball. We lost the first three games of the year, but then we went to Arizona and swept them, and we ended up having a good year. So did I.

To say that Pujols had a good first year is a bit of an understatement. After getting his first major-league hit in his first game, he went hitless in his next two games against the Colorado Rockies. Although many rookies might have panicked, thinking that their first hit would be their last, Pujols remained confident. "I was hitting the ball good, so I didn't get frustrated," he said, quoted in *Albert the Great*. "I knew what I could do. I just let it happen and had a good series in Arizona."

Again, to say he had a "good series" was surely an understatement. He had what can only be described as a *great* series, getting 7 hits in 14 at-bats. He hit his first home run, off Armando Reynoso. He drove in eight runs. He also got what can be described as one of the biggest hits of his career.

In the last game of the series, Pujols came to bat against superstar pitcher Randy Johnson, a sure future Hall of Famer. Pujols smashed a two-out, two-strike, two-run double that earned him his first photo in *Sports Illustrated* magazine. After just six games in the majors, Pujols was receiving national recognition.

Not only that, his teammates were beginning to appreciate how special Pujols was. As McGwire put it in *Albert the Great*, "When he bombed the double off the wall in center

After hitting a home run against the Milwaukee Brewers on May 28, 2001, Albert Pujols acknowledged the fans' applause at Busch Stadium in St. Louis. He was having a torrid start to his rookie season, hitting .370 in April and .333 in May with eight home runs each month.

against Randy Johnson, we all went, 'Uh-oh. We've got something here.'"

Returning to St. Louis for the team's first series at home, La Russa saw no reason to pull Pujols from the lineup. When Bobby Bonilla came off the disabled list a week into the season, it was obvious that Pujols was going to remain on the roster. The Cardinals' John Mabry was designated for assignment and his contract was sold to the Florida Marlins. Pujols had earned himself a permanent spot with the team. By the end of April, Pujols had eight home runs, tying the major-league record for rookies shared by Kent Hrbek and Carlos Delgado. He had a 13-game hitting streak. He was on fire as a player.

What impressed his teammates even more than his playing, however, was his composure. With McGwire still on the disabled list, La Russa moved Pujols to the cleanup position in the batting order, but it did not faze him for a moment. Hitting his first two-run home run, he was the obvious choice to be the National League Rookie of the Month.

Pujols's statistics at the end of April would have done a seasoned professional proud. He had a .370 batting average, along with 8 home runs and 27 RBIs. He had scored 18 runs and led the Cardinals in RBIs, home runs, runs, and games played.

His teammates were impressed by his attitude as well. As fellow Cardinal Larry Sutton said, quoted in *Albert the Great*, "He's the type of kid who will sit next to you and ask questions. He doesn't act presumptuous. He doesn't act like he's been in the big leagues for 10 years. He's in the cage 24 hours a day and wants to get better. That's all you can ask for from a young player."

Obviously, Pujols was not letting the attention go to his head. He knew he was still a rookie with a lot to learn, and he was not embarrassed to ask questions and get advice from his teammates.

Fast-starting rookies come and go, though. Many a young player starts the season with a bang and quickly fizzles, ending up back in the minors. There were those who predicted that Pujols would end up in that camp. They thought that he was benefiting from the fact that not many in the league had seen him play before. These skeptics thought that, once pitchers learned how he played, they would be able to pitch better against him. Bob Brenly, the manager of the Arizona Diamondbacks, was one of the doubters.

"We just don't know the kid," Brenly said at the time, quoted in *Albert the Great.* "The series we had in Arizona, we just had bad scouting reports. We ended up throwing the ball right where he likes it—a lot." Brenly, though, went on to praise Pujols as a player. "He's obviously a physically gifted young man. A lot of rookies come up at this level and feel overmatched. They're not sure if they belong or can compete at this level. Other rookies come up with that little edge, that confidence, that look in their eye that they belong. He certainly has that look."

As the weeks passed, it became more and more evident that Pujols was not going to be just a short-lived phenomenon, just another "player of the month." His May numbers were equally impressive. He hit .333, smashed another 8 home runs, and had 24 RBIs. In June, he hit .330 with 5 home runs and 15 RBIs, leading the team in both.

His teammates and coaches could not say enough nice things about him. Bonilla, the man whose injury allowed Pujols to get his shot with the team, said, quoted in *Albert the Great*, "I'm glad things worked out the way they did, because he had just as good a spring as anybody on the team, if not the best spring. He's going to do a lot more in this game."

It was Cardinals hitting coach Mike Easler who, like so many others, noted the distinctive sound of the ball hitting Pujols's bat. Easler said, quoted in *Albert the Great*:

> Only a few guys can make that sound. Willie Stargell, Dave Parker, Dave Winfield, Mike Schmidt. I'm talking about guys

like that. The ball just explodes off his bat, and he's talented enough that he can take his power swing and make adjustments and go the other way for a base hit.

I can tell him something in between at-bats about how a pitcher is trying to work him and he can make the adjustments just that quick. The next at-bat, he'll do exactly what you've talked to him about. It's just amazing how polished he is at such a young age. He has a quiet confidence that tells you he expects to be here for a long time.

ALL-STAR BREAK

As if to prove that he was in fact a mere mortal, though, Pujols went into the first prolonged batting slump of his career in July. There had been talk about Pujols making the All-Star team, even though he was not on the ballot. In the eight games leading to the All-Star break, Pujols hit just 2-for-33, including 0-for-12 with runners in scoring position, and his batting average dipped from .354 to .323. Despite that dry spell, his season numbers were just too strong to be ignored. Bobby Valentine, the manager of the National League team, named Pujols as a reserve for the All-Star Game. He was the first Cardinal rookie since pitcher Luis Arroyo in 1955 to be so honored.

Although many may have been surprised at his selection to the All-Star team, Pujols himself, while pleased, was not exactly amazed. As he said, quoted in Jeff Savage's *Albert Pujols*, "I don't know if I've surprised other people, but I'm not surprised. When you work hard, you can't be surprised. When you work hard, you get your goals." The values that his grandmother America passed on to him years earlier in the Dominican Republic obviously served him well.

Pujols replaced starter Jeff Kent during the game, becoming the first Cardinal rookie to actually play in the All-Star Game since third baseman Eddie Kazak in 1949. Even though he walked in his only at-bat, Pujols was thrilled to have had the opportunity to play in the game. It served as the culmination of a great first half of the season.

Pujols's cumulative numbers for the season's first half were certainly impressive. With 21 home runs, he had already tied the team's rookie record, with another half of the season left to play. At the All-Star break, he led all major-league rookies in

★ ★ ★ ★ ★ ☆

THE ST. LOUIS CARDINALS

The St. Louis Cardinals were originally formed as part of the American Association in 1882 and were known then as the "Brown Stockings," which was quickly shortened to "Browns." The Browns joined the National League in 1892, following the bankruptcy of the American Association. They were briefly called the Perfectos in 1899 before finally settling on their present name. The name "Cardinals" was reportedly inspired by a change in their uniform colors from brown to red, and since there was already a team called the "Reds" in Cincinnati, the St. Louis team became the "Cardinals."

Since then, the Cardinals have won 10 World Series, the most of any National League team and second only to the New York Yankees, who have won 26. Some of the team's best-known players over the years have been Rogers Hornsby, Dizzy Dean, Stan "The Man" Musial, Bob Gibson, Lou Brock, Joe Torre, Keith Hernandez, Ozzie Smith, Willie McGee, Mark McGwire, and today's Albert Pujols. Over the years, Cardinal fans have gained a reputation as the best and most knowledgeable in the game. Players have been known to tell other players that they have not played baseball until they have played baseball in St. Louis. To many, St. Louis is indeed "Baseball City, U.S.A."

home runs, RBIs, on-base percentage, and slugging percentage. It was a remarkable accomplishment.

And even more so when you consider how often manager La Russa moved him around defensively. In the season's first half, Pujols played 46 games at third base, 14 in right field, 13 at first base, six in left field, and two as a designated hitter. That Pujols could maintain his concentration as a batter with all these moves and with all the media attention he was receiving is a testament to his ability to focus on what is important to him—playing the game to the best of his abilities.

The Cardinals were stuck in third place at the All-Star break, playing .500 ball. The team caught fire in the second half of the season, entering the pennant race with a 20–10 record in the month of August. Pujols contributed to the team's surge, with a 17-game hitting streak and a massive 453-foot (138-meter) home run at Busch Stadium against the Marlins. The home run was the longest one hit by a Cardinal in 2001. On August 29, he hit his thirty-first home run of the season and became only the second Cardinal to drive in more than 100 runs in his rookie season.

At the end of August, the Cardinals were still six games out of first place in the National League Central Division, with a 73–61 record. A nine-game winning streak in September brought them firmly into contention for postseason play. It was obvious that Pujols would be the clear choice for Rookie of the Year honors, but he was also considered a possible winner of the Most Valuable Player award.

La Russa, the manager, thought that he was a viable candidate. As quoted in *Albert the Great,* he said, "I really believe the stats don't come anywhere close to telling the story of how this guy's played. That he's been able to maintain this for six months. . . . I don't care if you've been in the league for 10 years, he's had a phenomenal season.

"I've been fortunate and had some MVP performances. I think of [Carlton] Fisk, Harold Baines, José Canseco, Mark

McGwire, Rickey Henderson," La Russa added, mentioning the names of players he had managed. "But I don't know anybody who has had a better year than this guy. He's been as good as any I've been fortunate to see. . . . What this kid has done is the greatest performance of any position player I've ever seen."

Some people found it difficult to believe La Russa's comments: Pujols was better than McGwire? Better than Henderson? Pujols's play soon silenced them. "I had a couple of guys from the other league walk up to me who had read those comments I had made about Albert as a player," La Russa said, quoted in *Baseball Digest*. "And they said, 'I thought when you said those things you were exaggerating to make a point.' But then they said, 'We understand.'"

For Pujols, though, getting the Cardinals into the postseason was his No. 1 priority. His numbers continued to astonish, and in the ninth inning of an important game against Pittsburgh, Pujols broke a 5-5 tie with a grand slam—his first.

At the end of September, after another six-game winning streak, the Cardinals were tied with the Houston Astros for first with just five games to play. The two teams met in the final series of the season. The Astros won two of the three games, and both teams finished with identical 93–69 records. Houston was named the division champion because it had won the season series against the Cardinals. The Cardinals, though, were also eligible for postseason play by claiming the National League wild-card slot.

Due in no small part to his contribution to his team's success, Pujols once again appeared in the pages of *Sports Illustrated*. His list of accomplishments for his rookie season was noteworthy by any standards. For Pujols, they all paled in importance against his ultimate goal of helping his team make the play-offs and the World Series.

As he said, quoted in *Albert the Great*, "I don't try to think about records. I don't think about what Ted Williams did or what Frank Robinson did. I'm not trying to have a great year

Albert Pujols watched his first-inning, two-run homer leave the park during the second game of the 2001 National League Division Series against the Arizona Diamondbacks. The home run was one of only two hits that Pujols got in the five-game series, which the Diamondbacks won.

as a rookie setting records. I am trying to get my team into the play-offs and World Series. That's the only record that I want."

Unfortunately, it was not to be that season. The Cardinals did make the play-offs but lost in a five-game, first-round series to the Arizona Diamondbacks, who went on to win the World Series. Pujols fared poorly in the series, getting only two hits, one of them a home run, in 18 at-bats. Even this less-than-stellar performance could do nothing to lessen his triumphant rookie season.

For despite the fine season posted by other Cardinal players, it was clear that Pujols was the real story in St. Louis. In 161 games, he led the Cards with a .329 batting average, 194 hits, 37 homers, 47 doubles, 130 RBIs, and 112 runs scored.

He was only the fifth rookie to lead the Cardinals in batting average for a season, the first since 1974. He was only the seventh rookie to lead the team in homers, the first since 1990. He was only the third rookie to lead the team in RBIs, the first since 1933. The only other rookie to lead the team in all three Triple Crown categories was the legendary Rogers Hornsby in 1916.

Pujols was also only the fourth rookie in baseball history, and the first in the National League, to hit .300 with 30 home runs, 100 RBIs, and 100 runs scored, a feat matched by only Cleveland's Hal Trosky in 1934, Boston's Ted Williams in 1939, and Boston's Walt Dropo in 1950.

Pujols set Cardinal rookie records for home runs, doubles, RBIs, extra-base hits, runs, and total bases. He established new National League rookie records for RBIs, extra-base hits, and total bases. He finished in the National League's top 10 in batting average, RBIs, multi-hit games, total bases, doubles, on-base percentage, slugging percentage, extra-base hits, and game-winning RBIs.

It was, in other words, a season for the record books, and arguably the greatest rookie season in baseball history. Albert

The fans at Busch Stadium gave Albert Pujols a standing ovation during his at-bat in the seventh inning of a game against the Brewers on
September 19, 2001. Earlier in the game, he had broken the National
League single-season rookie record for RBIs. He set several other
rookie records and was named the league's Rookie of the Year.

Pujols was the unanimous choice as the National League Rookie of the Year, just the ninth unanimous selection in league history. He finished fourth in the MVP-award balloting, losing to Barry Bonds, who that year broke the record for home runs in a single season with 73.

Pujols was well aware that one great season did not make a career. He knew that next year, pitchers would be watching for him, and fans and critics would be ready to pounce on any sign of slipping. La Russa warned him about the potential problems he could face as his career in the majors progressed, quoted in *Albert the Great*:

> He could do this for a long time. The two biggest issues that could get in the way of him having a great career are first, that he's a big guy. We saw in spring training that he had a really good winter training and stayed in shape. He was quick. The older you get, the tougher it is to carry weight. So he will have to keep up that kind of work.
>
> Second, maybe most important, is the atmosphere today in the major leagues that if a guy is successful, even if he is just a little successful, much less incredibly successful, he will face a lot of pressure to focus on [outside influences].

Pujols was well aware of the pitfalls that go with being a baseball superstar. The demands on your time, the allure of fame, the temptations of alcohol, drugs, and women can all distract from what makes you famous in the first place—playing baseball. Going into his second season, Pujols was determined to stay true to himself as a human being and as an athlete and avoid being labeled a one-season wonder.

Would He
Be a Fluke?

Albert Pujols prepared for his second season in the majors as he always prepared for the game—waking up early every morning for batting practice and arduous weight training. He knew that this workout was essential to keep himself in top form, able to perform at his best for the entire season.

His teammates all admired and were inspired by Pujols's drive to be the best. Cardinal catcher Mike Matheny commented in *Albert the Great*, "You look at how far he has come as a player in two years. He's a central player on this team. There are people coming at him from every angle who want something from him. To his credit, he's able to keep his focus. Some people may have trouble understanding that, but there's probably no way he can make everyone happy."

Pujols's goal was to make himself happy. The only way he could do that was to help his team make it to the play-offs and then to the World Series. To achieve that goal, he was determined to be better as a player, to improve upon, if possible, his phenomenal rookie season.

Many players, having the success that Pujols had, and hearing from everyone around them how great they were, would be content to maintain their play at the same level they had. Not Pujols. He was always watching other hitters, watching pitchers, taking mental notes, learning from everything he saw. As he once said, quoted in *Albert the Great*, "I learn something every time I walk into a park. You learn from your mistakes and things that happen. Every day, you learn something new, and that's what you want to do to get better and better." For Pujols, the day he stops learning is the day he stops improving.

Pujols is quick to say that hard work and natural talent are just part of his success. Religion is at the center of his and Deidre's life. For them, God is first, and everything else, even baseball, is a distant second. As Pujols says on his foundation's Web site (http://www.pujolsfamilyfoundation.org), "Growing up in the Dominican Republic, I lived to play baseball. My wife, Deidre . . . shared how much Jesus loved me. I realized I needed more than religion. I needed a Savior. Jesus Christ wanted a personal relationship with me." On November 13, 1998, Pujols made what he called "the best decision of my life." On that day, as it says on his Web site, "he gave his heart to Jesus Christ and asked him to become the Lord of his life."

Pujols credits his success as a ballplayer to his relationship with God. "People ask me if I believe how quickly my career has taken off. I just tell them that Jesus Christ is my strength. God has blessed me, and I will continue to do my best for Him. That is more important than anything I could ever do in baseball."

Deidre Pujols agrees that all of her husband's accomplishments come from God. "Albert and I recognize that his awesome talent is a gift from God, and because of that belief, our lives have been blessed beyond belief," she is quoted as saying on the family foundation Web site.

But if it was religion that gave Pujols his strength and support, he also knew how fortunate he was to have made it as a baseball player, and he was smart enough to know that it would take hard work to keep himself on top.

As he said, quoted in *Albert the Great*, "I don't want to throw this opportunity away. I don't want to be lazy in this game. I don't want to be cocky. I don't want to think that I'm the best. I always want to be humble and be the same guy I was three or four years ago, when I signed, through the minor leagues and here in the big leagues."

While Pujols prepared himself mentally and physically for the new season, the Cardinals did the same, hoping for another exciting year. The club signed first baseman Tino Martinez, brought in Jason Isringhausen as the new closing pitcher, and welcomed new starting pitcher Woody Williams, who had been acquired late in the 2001 season. Outside of these three additions, the rest of the lineup looked pretty much the same, with one exception. Mark McGwire, as expected, had officially announced his retirement.

THE 2002 SEASON

When the regular season began, Pujols, for the first time in his career, appeared to be human after all. National League pitchers seemed to have his number, driving him off the plate as he struggled to hold his ground. His batting average in the first half of the season did not rise much higher than .280, and some began to think that he was, in fact, a one-season wonder.

Pujols remained confident, though. He knew that he was still hitting well when it counted, with runners in scoring position. He knew that his power numbers were still strong and that his play was improving in both the infield and the outfield.

Kansas City Royals catcher Brent Mayne tried to tag out Albert Pujols during a game on June 9, 2002. Pujols was called safe as he scored from third on a wild pitch by Miguel Asencio *(left)*. Pujols had a lackluster first half of the season, and some began to think he might be a one-season wonder.

(He was playing left field, first base, and third base.) He was confident that, if he did not panic and kept doing what he was doing, his numbers would improve.

At the same time, the team was also having a rough first half of the season. On June 18, 2002, the Cardinals' much beloved longtime announcer, Jack Buck, passed away. Then, just four days later, pitcher Darryl Kile, whose 16–11 record in 2001 had helped propel the team into the play-offs, was found in his bed, dead of a heart attack at the age of 33. He was the first active major-league player to die during the regular season since the Yankees' Thurman Munson died in a plane crash in 1979.

The loss of a popular pitcher hit the Cardinals and their fans extremely hard. Many expected that the team would not be able to recover mentally and emotionally from the loss. Instead, the team regrouped, dedicating the remainder of the season to Kile's memory, vowing to win it "for Darryl."

By the end of the season, the team was sitting firmly in first place in the Central Division, with a record of 97–65. In a fitting tribute to their fallen teammate, when the Cardinals clinched the division in a game against Kile's old team, the Houston Astros, Pujols carried out Kile's No. 57 jersey, on a hanger, to the celebration on the field.

Indeed, it was Pujols's strong second half that keyed the team's ascent in the standings. After the All-Star break, he batted .335 with a league-leading 61 RBIs, and he ended the regular season as one of four National League players in the top 10 in the Triple Crown categories—batting average, home runs, and RBIs. (The others were Barry Bonds and Jeff Kent, both of the San Francisco Giants, and Vladimir Guerrero of the Montreal Expos.)

In fact, even after his shaky start, Pujols ended up leading his team in batting average, home runs, RBIs, and runs, just as he had in his rookie season. In the process, he became the first player in the history of Major League Baseball to hit at least .300 with 30 home runs, 100 RBIs, and 100 runs scored in each of his first two seasons.

His numbers were beginning to earn comparisons to some of baseball's best. Pujols became the first hitter since the great Ted Williams in 1939 and 1940 to have more than 250 RBIs in his first two years in the majors. Only two other players, Joe DiMaggio and Dale Alexander, had previously achieved the same feat.

In 2002, Pujols climbed from fourth place to second place in the balloting for the Most Valuable Player, but once again

Albert Pujols held up the jersey of teammate Darryl Kile after the Cardinals clinched the National League Central Division title with a win over Houston on September 20, 2002. Kile, a pitcher with the Cardinals, died earlier in the season of a heart attack.

he lost the coveted award to Barry Bonds. The awards and records, however, were not what mattered to him. What did was helping his team reach the World Series. As he said, quoted in Jeff Savage's *Albert Pujols*, "I don't worry about winning the MVP, the batting title, or home runs. I don't think about that stuff. If you start putting those things in your head, you just put pressure on yourself. You don't want to do that. You want to keep your mind clear. I just want to get ready to help the team out."

Although Pujols was beginning to be compared to the greats, Barry Bonds disagreed. According to an article by Matt McHale in *Baseball Digest*, Bonds felt that Pujols lacked the foot speed to be a great all-around player. Besides, as Bonds pointed out in an interview with St. Louis TV station KDSK, "So much about the comparisons are subjective. But longevity is the biggest part of any discussion. After my first MVP-type season, if I had gotten hurt or never played again, what would they say about my career? Maybe something about my father or maybe something about my potential. That's it."

Pujols, though, refused to get into any debate with Bonds. His eye was on the National League Division Series against the Arizona Diamondbacks. Still smarting from their defeat at the hands of the Diamondbacks in the 2001 play-offs, the Cardinals were out to avenge their loss.

Avenge it they did, defeating the Diamondbacks in a three-game sweep. Pujols, who had three hits including a triple, batted a solid .300, contributing greatly to the team's success.

The Cardinals next squared off against the San Francisco Giants in the National League Championship Series. The series was a publicist's dream, featuring a showdown between two of the game's most dangerous and powerful hitters— Pujols and Bonds. St. Louis lost the series in five games. A major factor in the Cardinals' defeat was the loss of newly acquired third baseman Scott Rolen to injury. Pujols himself started well, getting a homer off Kirk Rueter in Game 1, but he saw fewer and fewer good pitches as the series progressed. Neither Pujols nor Bonds, however, lit it up during the series—Pujols batted .263 with one home run, while Bonds hit .273, also with one homer.

Rolen, who had played against the Cardinals before joining the team, gained new respect for Pujols while watching him play on a daily basis. As he said, quoted in *Albert the Great*:

★ ★ ★ ★ ☆

ONE-SEASON WONDERS

Although Albert Pujols was able to avoid being called a "one-season wonder," others have not been so lucky. These players had great rookie seasons and seemed headed for stardom, but instead they faded quickly, soon to be forgotten.

Any such list of players would have to include John Paciorek of the Houston Colt 45s, who played one game in the majors, on September 29, 1963. In that game, he had three hits and two walks, drove in three runs, and scored four runs, but because of back problems, he never made it back to the majors. Or Baltimore Orioles rookie Wally Bunker, 19, who pitched a one-hitter in his first start. Bunker went on to win his first six starts, pitching another one-hitter in the process, and he finished the 1964 season with a 19–5 record and 2.69 ERA. He never regained his rookie form, though, and finished his nine-year career with a 60–52 record. Or Bob Hamelin, who in the strike-shortened season of 1994 hit 24 home runs with a .282 batting average and 65 RBIs, winning the American League Rookie of the Year award. He went on to hit .168 in his second season and was out of baseball by 1998.

You see him twice a year and you figure you're catching him when he's hot. When you're on the same team, you realize he's like that every day. You think he has to cool off sometimes, but he doesn't. He's that good. He has a knack of controlling the at-bat instead of the pitcher controlling the at-bat. The pitcher needs to make adjustments. The other thing is, he has the ability of knowing where that bat head is and getting that bat head to the ball. Barry [Bonds] hits so many balls on the barrel. That's the way Albert is. You can

☆ ☆ ☆ ☆ ☆ ☆

Joe Charboneau of the Cleveland Indians was probably best known as a player who would celebrate after a game by opening a beer bottle with his eye socket and then drinking the beer with a straw through his nose. In his first game as a rookie in 1980, he hit a single, a double, and a three-run homer. He finished the season with 23 home runs, 87 RBIs, and a batting average of .289. After playing only 70 more games in the majors over the next two seasons, his career was over.

Perhaps the most famous "one-season wonder" was the Detroit Tigers pitcher Mark "The Bird" Fidrych. In 1976, his rookie year, he captured the imagination of baseball fans throughout the country, going 19–9 with a 2.34 ERA. That year was his only complete season, as arm problems led to an unremarkable 10–10 record for the remaining four years of his career.

Players like these remind us that fame is, indeed, fleeting and that it takes more than one or two great seasons to have a great career.

Starting pitcher Matt Morris *(top)* and Albert Pujols appear stunned after the Cardinals lost the 2002 National League Championship Series to the San Francisco Giants. Pujols said he and his teammates would have to put the defeat behind them as they moved into the 2003 season.

throw him an inside pitch, and he might hit a home run to right field. He's not concerned about pulling the ball.

Tony Gwynn, the San Diego Padres Hall of Famer who is widely considered to be one of the best hitters in history, had this to say about Pujols, quoted on the *Baseball Almanac* Web site, "Pujols is a new breed of player in that he is both versatile in the field and disciplined at the plate. He is athletic enough to play first base, third base, or either corner outfield position. And in only his second season, Pujols is one of the game's best young hitters. Because his numbers are so good, he makes you forget that he is only 22."

Anyone watching Pujols play through his first two seasons in the major leagues had to be impressed. And although Pujols was undoubtedly disappointed at his team's failure to reach the World Series, he could not help but be proud of his own accomplishments. In his first two years as a St. Louis Cardinal, he had established himself as one of baseball's true superstars, having had perhaps the most successful start to a baseball career in history. Still, however, the eyes of everyone who watched baseball continued to be on him.

Expectations were sky-high for the 2003 season. But would the disappointing end to the 2002 play-offs cast a shadow over the players? Pujols knew that, to win in 2003, he and his team would have to put the 2002 loss behind them. As quoted on the *Baseball Almanac* Web site, Pujols said, "I thought about it a lot [losing the 2002 NLCS]. It's something you have to go home and wrap it up because if you keep thinking about it, you're going to take that to spring training and you're not going to be able to concentrate on your work."

Pujols is famous for his skill at focusing on the task at hand. Would Pujols be able to put the 2002 play-offs behind him, and come out next season and satisfy his fans, his team, and, most of all, himself?

Chasing
the Series

With the beginning of the 2003 season, Albert Pujols was being acknowledged as a true baseball superstar. He was at the heart of a powerful batting order in St. Louis. Jim Edmonds, Tino Martinez, Scott Rolen, and Edgar Rentería provided him with plenty of support in the lineup, making it a list of hitters any pitcher worried about facing. The team's biggest weakness was its pitching: Woody Williams and Matt Morris were strong pitchers, but both also had a history of arm problems. The rest of the pitching staff was a mix of older pitchers approaching the end of their careers and young pitchers just breaking in. Also, with closer Jason Isringhausen coming back from an injury, the Cardinals' bullpen was on shaky ground, to say the least.

As it turned out, it was the Cardinals' pitching that ultimately spelled the end of the team's play-off hopes for 2003. The team managed to stay near the top of the division along with the Cubs and Astros through the first half of the season, thanks largely to the high-scoring offense. When Morris missed part of the season with an elbow injury, however, Williams alone was not enough to hold the pitching staff together. As the season progressed, the team faded from serious contention for postseason play after losing a September series to Chicago. The Cardinals finished in third place in the National League Central with a record of 85–77, just three games behind the champion Chicago Cubs, ending the team's three-year run of play-off appearances.

Although the Cardinals' season was disappointing, Pujols himself continued to play like a man possessed. As good as his numbers were in his first two seasons, Pujols was determined to improve upon them in 2003. To do so, he continued to adjust his game to that of opposing pitchers. As he said, quoted in *Albert the Great*, "That's how you become a good hitter, when you can tell yourself what you're doing wrong and correct it the next at-bat. You don't want to do the same thing in three at-bats . . . then do something different in the last at-bat. By then, it's too late.

"You want to make adjustments your first at-bat," he added. "You don't have to wait until somebody else corrects it. Sometimes it's better for people outside to say something, but 90 percent of the time I know what I'm doing wrong. I don't do much with my arms and legs. I'm quiet."

Quiet, but effective. In the first half of the season, he hit .368 with 27 home runs and 86 RBIs. These are numbers that most players would be delighted to have amassed over an entire season. It came as no surprise, then, that Pujols was elected to play in the 2003 All-Star Game, leading all National

League players with more than 2 million votes in balloting by the fans.

Despite being robbed of a hit in the game because of an outstanding fielding play by Ichiro Suzuki, Pujols still managed to make his presence known. During the Home Run Derby the day before the game, Pujols smashed a record-tying 14 homers in the semifinal round, before losing 9-8 to Anaheim's Garret Anderson in the final.

☆ ☆ ☆ ☆ ☆ ☆

HOME RUN DERBY

If it is true that most baseball fans love nothing more than seeing a ball hit out of the park, then few events are more popular than the Home Run Derby, held annually just before the All-Star Game. It is a contest among the major leagues' top home-run hitters to see who, in fact, can hit the most home runs.

Eight players are selected for the Home Run Derby. These eight compete in a traditional play-off system, in which the players with the most home runs advance to the next round. Each player gets 10 "outs" per round—in this case, an out is defined as any swing that is not a home run. If a tie exists between players at the end of any round, the number of regular-season home runs by the All-Star break is the first tiebreaker and the distance of the longest home run in the first round is the second tiebreaker. The event is broadcast live—the 2006 Derby lasted nearly three hours.

The 2007 Home Run Derby was won by Vladimir Guerrero of the Los Angeles Angels of Anaheim, who defeated Alex Ríos of Toronto in the final round. Albert Pujols made it to the semifinals. In his only other appearance in the Home Run Derby, Pujols finished second in 2003.

Albert Pujols watched one of his hits soar during the Home Run Derby at U.S. Cellular Field in Chicago on July 14, 2003. He tied a record with 14 home runs in the semifinal round, though he lost the derby in the final.

Other players, both teammates as well as opposing pitchers, continued to have nothing but praise for Pujols's abilities. Cardinals first baseman Tino Martinez said, quoted in *Albert the Great*: "It's gotten to the point where you don't even marvel anymore. You just kind of expect it. Yeah, you expect him to hit home runs. You expect him to drive in runs, and you expect him to have great at-bats every time. We're just used to seeing it.

"I've played with great, great players, guys who put up some good numbers. But I've never seen a guy as focused as he is. The focus is unbelievable." Despite the constant accolades, Pujols knew that staying great was a constant test. "I've got to go out and prove it every day," he is quoted as saying in Jeff Savage's *Albert Pujols.*

"God gave me this natural ability," Pujols said, quoted in *Albert the Great.* "But it's even better when you work hard and you put those two things together. (Then) it's unbelievable. . . . I've been blessed. I don't know how. The main thing is I can read a pitcher. I can make adjustments. People wonder how I am able to do that. I don't know. I can't explain. . . . I try to see the ball and have a plan."

Many observers feel that the other major components of Pujols's success are his quick hands and strong arms. These give him the ability to come around on the ball fast enough so that, even on an inside pitch, he hits it strongly and squarely, giving it that Pujols "whack" and allowing it to stay in fair territory.

Like most players, Pujols is uncomfortable talking about the mechanics of his swing, but he does agree that his performance is built around his hands.

"The key to hitting is hands," he said, quoted in *Albert the Great.* "You leave your hands back so even if you jump at the ball, your hands are back. If it's a breaking ball, you can still put a good swing on it. Sometimes you're going to get fooled on a breaking ball. Then you adjust to the next pitch. But what's most important is for my hands to be in the right position for me to drive the ball.

"If it's away, I can drive the ball away. If it's inside, I can pull the ball down the line."

Words like that coming from other players would sound like boasting, but Pujols makes them sound like a simple statement of fact. And he backs up his talk with numbers that continue to amaze. His statistics at the end of the 2003 season were no exception.

Pujols saw fewer and fewer pitches to hit as the season progressed, with pitchers willing to take their chances throwing to Rolen and Rentería on either side of him in the lineup. Still, he had a 30-game hitting streak, the longest by a Cardinal since Stan Musial in 1950. Pujols's streak was broken only when he was hit with a bad case of the flu.

In fact, his 2003 season was one of the finest in Cardinal history. Pujols hit .359 with 43 home runs, 124 RBIs, and 137 runs scored. He totaled 212 hits, including 51 doubles. He won his first National League batting title, just edging out Colorado's Todd Helton. At 23, he was the youngest player to win the title since the Dodgers' Tommy Davis in 1962. And perhaps most impressive, in 685 appearances at the plate, he struck out only 65 times.

Pujols led the majors, both the National and American Leagues, in runs scored, doubles, extra-base hits, and total bases. He even became only the second player in Cardinal history to have 40 home runs and 200 hits in the same season, a feat not accomplished since Rogers Hornsby did it back in 1922.

Although Pujols's numbers were certainly worthy of a Most Valuable Player award, once again he came in second place behind San Francisco Giants slugger Barry Bonds. Bonds continued to express his doubts about Pujols's abilities, stating that only longevity as a player was a true test of greatness.

"Who does he compare to?" Bonds repeated a question, quoted in *Albert the Great*. "Alex Rodriguez, Ken Griffey, Jr., those types of players. It took me a little longer. I played a couple of extra years before I understood the game. They learned it a lot faster than I did, within about a three-year span.

"Give Pujols time. I tell people a story about a kid who's been like my brother forever in this game of baseball, and happens to have had a lot of injuries, and no one ever talks

Albert Pujols and Barry Bonds met up on the field before a game on June 30, 2003, at Busch Stadium in St. Louis. Bonds has said that longevity is a key to greatness and it is too soon to talk about how Pujols stacks up against the top names in the sport. Pujols pays no mind to Bonds's comments.

about Junior [Ken Griffey] anymore. So before you put Pujols on that pedestal, let him play for a while first, because he's not there yet."

Pujols just shrugged off Bonds's criticisms, as he does all negative comments. "I heard something about it, but hey, whatever he said it's not in my mind," he said in an article by

Matt McHale in *Baseball Digest*. "I don't care what he says or what other people say. I just try to concentrate."

Although Pujols may not have been "there" yet, his cumulative numbers for his first three seasons in the majors showed he was well on his way. In 2003, Pujols tied Ralph Kiner for the record of most home runs in the first three years of major-league play, with 114. He joined Mark McGwire and José Canseco as the only players in history to hit 30 or more home runs in each of the first three years of their careers. He also became the only player in major-league history to hit 30 home runs, drive in 100 runs, and score 100 runs in each of his first three seasons. Any way you look at it, his first three years were impressive.

For Pujols, though, the only statistics that really mattered were the team wins that led to an appearance in the World Series. Anything else was not important. "I'm a teammate guy, so whatever I can do to help my team win . . . that's what I want to do," Pujols is quoted as saying on the *Baseball Almanac* Web site.

Moving into the winter break, Pujols had many things to do. Negotiations for a new contract were beginning with the Cardinals. Spending time with his wife, Deidre, and his children, Isabella and A.J., were top priorities. Always lurking in the back of his mind were his goals for 2004—keeping fit, improving as a player, and helping his team reach the World Series.

8

The Chase Continues

As the 2004 season began, expectations for the Cardinals were low. Many baseball writers predicted that the team would finish no better than third place in the National League Central Division. The writers felt that both the pitching-rich Chicago Cubs and Houston Astros would have better seasons. Once again, the Cardinals' lack of strong pitching was seen as the team's Achilles' heel. Even though Chris Carpenter, Jason Marquis, and Jeff Suppan had joined Matt Morris and Woody Williams on the Cardinals' pitching staff, no one expected the rotation to deliver a full season of quality pitching.

The team's offense, of course, was another matter. Albert Pujols, Jim Edmonds, Scott Rolen, and Edgar Rentería were all healthy and ready to do what was expected of them. The team had also made a couple of key pick-ups for the daily lineup, including Tony Womack and Reggie Sanders.

Pujols was eager to start another run for the pennant. Shortly before the season began, he had signed a seven-year contract worth $100 million. The contract, which earned him the title of "the richest player in the storied history of the Cardinals," must have been particularly sweet for Pujols. It is easy to imagine him thinking back to his days playing baseball on the streets of Santo Domingo, when he was unable to afford even basic equipment, and realizing just how far he had come.

With a new contract to live up to, though, Pujols knew that he could not let himself or his teammates down. He prepared for the season as he always did, training hard and pushing himself to the utmost.

On most mornings, he arrived at his favorite gym, located in a nondescript warehouse in Pleasant Valley, Missouri. Pujols has known the gym's owner, Chris Mihlfeld, since his days at Maple Woods Community College, when Pujols was just 18. With assistance from Pujols, Mihlfeld was able to lease and equip his gym, a space that allows Pujols and Mihlfeld to train in private. Mihlfeld also trains a few other professional ballplayers.

Pujols typically begins his day of training by jumping rope and stretching; then he begins to lift weights, starting light and gradually working up to dumbbell presses of 85 pounds (38.5 kilograms) for each arm while lying flat on a bench. After lifting weights for nearly an hour and a half, he takes a lunch break and then begins batting practice. (An interesting note is that Pujols does not take any batting practice for the first five weeks of the off-season, allowing his body to repair itself from the normal wear and tear of playing a regular season of baseball.)

Beginning with soft underhand pitches, Mihlfeld gradually picks up the pace until, for example, Pujols is hitting line drives off the outside corner of the plate into right field for 20 straight

When Albert Pujols gets into his stance, he holds his hands level with his right ear and flaps his elbows a few times. Doing so relaxes Pujols. "I don't want to be too stiff, because then my hands won't be as quick," Pujols told an interviewer.

minutes. In his stance, as Daniel G. Habib pointed out in his *Sports Illustrated* article "A Swing of Beauty," Pujols splays his legs at the knees, resting about 60 percent of his body weight on his back foot. He then brings his hands up level with his right ear and flaps his elbows three or four times, always keeping the bat upright.

That move relaxes his body and his hands, because, as he told Habib: "I don't want to be too stiff, because then my hands won't be as quick." Habib noted that Pujols does not stride forward when he swings. Instead, his front foot curls inward so that he stands pigeon-toed when the ball hits the bat, driving with his hips. "I'm trying to slow my body down and slow my swing down, use my hands and trust my hands. I just try to trust my hands and leave it nice and quiet."

This is a huge part of Pujols's success (as well as that of other star athletes). Constant practice, constant repetition of the *mechanics* of hitting, make it second nature, just as, for example, walking is to a non-athlete. Hitting tens of thousands of balls in practice allows the movement to become automatic.

Never completely satisfied, always looking for ways to improve his swing, Pujols is constantly studying his game. The Cardinals have cameras set up in center field and along the first- and third-base lines, allowing batters to review their swings from every angle. After every at-bat, Pujols watches the video, making sure that all the habits that he practiced over and over during the off-season—the placement of his hands, the movement of his hips, the position of his head—are right where he wants them to be. Only through this constant self-scrutiny is Pujols able to maintain his form over the entire season.

Although Pujols is always studying his batting technique, he does not feel comfortable talking or even bragging about it. "It's whatever I feel comfortable with. I don't try to be a scientific baseball batter or a freaking genius baseball hitter," he told Habib. All he wants to be is the *best* baseball hitter.

THE 2004 SEASON

To the surprise of few, the Cardinals got off to a slow start in 2004, compiling a 27–23 record by the end of May. To the surprise of many, though, Pujols, perhaps feeling the pressure of being the "$100 million man," got off to a slow start as well. Or perhaps it was a result of a sore hamstring. In either case, he hit "only" .287 in April, with 7 home runs and 17 RBIs. Most hitters would be happy with those numbers, but it was the first month he had hit below .300 since June 2002.

The season, though, quickly began to turn around for both Pujols and his team. (Could there be a connection?) In a May contest against the Cubs at Wrigley Field in Chicago, Pujols and Edmonds hit back-to-back home runs in the fifth inning, with the Cardinals getting a hard-fought 7-6 victory. After that win, the team never looked back.

From June 1 to the All-Star break, the Cardinals won 27 of 37 games and built a seven-game lead in their division. In July and August, the team went an incredible 41–12, destroying the hopes of every other team in the National League Central, and it was Pujols who was perhaps most responsible for this success. In 24 games in July, he hit .374 with 9 home runs and 22 RBIs. In August, he hit .351 with 12 home runs and 29 RBIs in 27 games.

His bat was on fire. On July 20 in Chicago, Pujols played one of the best offensive games of his career, hitting three home runs and driving in five runs. It was the first three-homer game by a Cardinal since Mark McGwire managed the same feat in 2000.

Again, though, despite all his personal achievements, despite the records broken, what impressed his teammates and his manager was Pujols's determination to put the needs of the team first.

As his manager Tony La Russa said, quoted in *Albert the Great*, "The best thing about Albert is he's playing to win. He's playing for a ring for himself, his teammates, and

Albert Pujols picked off Rob Mackowiak of the Pittsburgh Pirates at first base during a game in June 2004. Pujols took the throw from Cardinals catcher Yadier Molina. In 2004, Pujols became the Cardinals' regular first baseman.

the Cardinals fans. That's what I admire about him most. Nothing else is a close second. The true winning player lets the numbers, the stats, and the money happen. That's what he does."

This is not to say that, despite his humility as a player, he is not fully aware of his status as a superstar. Despite finishing second in the Home Run Derby at the 2003 All-Star Game, Pujols was not invited to participate in the 2004 Home Run Derby. When other players withdrew from the derby because of injuries or other reasons, Pujols was asked if he would participate. Not willing to appear as a sort of afterthought, he politely declined. He did play in the All-Star Game, however, collecting his first two hits, both doubles.

Pujols's hot streak continued through the entire season. On August 3, he smashed his thirtieth home run of the season. With that first-inning blast, he became the only player in baseball history to hit 30 or more home runs in each of the first four years of his career. As expected, Pujols was pleased but underwhelmed. "I'm glad I'm the only guy, but there's a lot of the season left. I just want to stay consistent. It's just a home run." As always, Pujols was looking ahead.

And there was much more to come. On August 29, at Pittsburgh, Pujols blasted his fortieth home run of the year, and with that same hit, drove in his 100th run of the season. It was the second year in a row that Pujols had hit 40 home runs and his fourth year in a row that he had 100 RBIs, an achievement that placed his name among those of the greats.

Again, Pujols was not too impressed and was definitely not ready to rest on his laurels. Quoted in *Albert the Great,* he said, "It's awesome. Forty and 100 is tough to do at this level, but I don't care what kind of numbers I put up or who they compare me to. I just want to be a winner. When you start thinking about your numbers and what you've done in the big leagues, that's when you start feeling comfortable, and I don't want to do that."

With another important benchmark reached on September 26, it was apparent that Pujols was doing anything but relaxing and feeling comfortable. On that date, Pujols surpassed the 500-RBI career mark, becoming the first player in 62 years to amass that many RBIs in just four seasons in the majors. The only other players to achieve that feat were Ted Williams and Joe DiMaggio—by any standards, two of the greatest players ever. Pujols reacted in typical fashion, saying that the last four years had been great, but he was just taking it one year at a time. Indeed, for Pujols, it is one game at a time.

At the end of the regular season, Pujols's numbers demonstrated once again why he is perhaps considered baseball's best player. With a batting average of .331, a career-high 46 home runs, 51 doubles, 389 total bases, and only 52 strikeouts, he was the offensive powerhouse that propelled the Cardinals to a record of 105–57 and an astonishing 13-game lead in their division. As the play-offs began, all eight position players were healthy, and hopes were high that the Cardinals could win their first World Series since 1982. The first step would be to defeat the Los Angeles Dodgers.

THE PLAY-OFFS

Pujols set the pace for the Cardinals in the first game of the National League Division Series by homering off Odalis Pérez in his first at-bat in the first inning. In that same game, he also singled and scored in a five-run third inning that helped the Cardinals to an 8-3 victory. With another win the following night, the Cardinals flew to Los Angeles leading two games to none in the best-of-five series.

The Cardinals were shut out by José Lima in the third game. In the fourth game, though, Pujols's home run in the fourth inning helped carry the team into the National League Championship Series for the second time in three years. After losing to the San Francisco Giants in 2002, Pujols was determined that his team would defeat the Houston Astros in the 2004 series.

Once again, Pujols led the way in the first game, hitting a two-run homer in the first inning, propelling the Cardinals on to a 10-7 victory. His streak continued in the second game, with two singles and a run scored before he broke a 4-4 tie in the eighth inning with another home run, giving the Cards a 6-4 win.

With the Cards holding a two-games-to-none lead, the series moved to Houston, where the Astros had not lost a game in more than a month. Unfortunately for the Cardinals, the Astros' home streak continued, with the team winning all three games. Pujols had a home run and three RBIs at Minute Maid Park, but it was not enough. The championship series would go back to St. Louis with the Cards trailing three games to two.

Facing elimination, the Cardinals fought back hard. In the bottom of the first inning, Pujols blasted his sixth home run of the postseason with Tony Womack on second, putting the Cardinals ahead, 2-1. At his next at-bat in the third inning, Pujols's leadoff double triggered a two-run rally that put the Cardinals ahead, 4-2.

The Astros came fighting back and tied the game in the ninth inning. Finally in the twelfth inning, with the game still tied, relief pitcher Dan Miceli decided to walk Pujols. Jim Edmonds came up one out later and smashed a two-run homer, giving the Cardinals the win and forcing a seventh and final game.

In *Albert the Great,* Pujols talked about how the game demonstrated the team's determination to win. "When you take things for granted, that's when it slips away from you. We don't want that to happen. We don't want to wait until next year. One-hundred sixty-two games and wait and see if we're going to be in this situation. There's one game away to get us to the next level. We're going to try to make it happen."

Of course, the Astros were determined to make sure that it *wouldn't* happen, and their top pitcher, future Hall of Famer Roger Clemens, would be on the mound for Game 7. By the sixth inning, the Astros were ahead 2-1 and the Cards were just 10 outs away from being eliminated. Up to bat came Pujols. Roger Cedeño, the tying run, was on second.

Pujols's batting record against Clemens was not particularly impressive. He was 2-for-14 lifetime against the pitching legend and 0-for-5 in the series. Given this, the decision was made by Clemens and Astros manager Phil Garner to pitch

Scott Rolen and Albert Pujols celebrated after Rolen's home run in Game 7 of the 2004 National League Championship Series. Pujols scored on Rolen's home run, which gave the Cardinals the victory and the National League pennant. The win came against Roger Clemens *(foreground)*, the Astros' ace.

to Pujols. Clemens threw three straight fastballs, bringing the count to 1-2. With two strikes against him, Pujols was in an unenviable position. Was Clemens going to bring Pujols's series record against him to 0-for-6?

Not a chance. On Clemens's next pitch, Pujols smashed it into the left-field corner for a double that scored Cedeño from second, tying the game. For Pujols, the hit would be one of the highlights of his career. As he said later, quoted in *Albert the Great,* "I'm going to keep dreaming about it for the next couple

☆ ☆ ☆ ☆ ☆ ☆

ROGER CLEMENS

The nemesis of many a great hitter, including Albert Pujols, Roger Clemens (born August 4, 1962, in Dayton, Ohio) has been one of the pre-eminent major-league pitchers of the 1980s, 1990s, and 2000s. Nicknamed "The Rocket," he is widely considered to be one of the greatest pitchers of all time. He has won seven Cy Young Awards—more than any other pitcher.

Clemens made his major-league debut in 1984 with the Boston Red Sox, with whom he played for 13 seasons. In 1986, he had a record of 24–4 in helping to lead the Red Sox to the World Series (they lost to the New York Mets in a heartbreaking seven-game series). That year, Clemens was named the American League Most Valuable Player and he won the first of his Cy Young Awards.

Also in 1986, he became the first pitcher to strike out 20 batters in a nine-inning game. He accomplished this feat against the Seattle Mariners. Ten years later, he did it again, striking out 20 against the Detroit Tigers. Still, after the 1996 season, Red Sox general manager Dan Duquette, thinking that Clemens's best days were behind him, said that he was "in the of weeks. I didn't want to try to do too much, just see a good pitch to hit. He didn't make a bad pitch, just thank the Lord my hands came through."

On Clemens's next pitch, Scott Rolen hit a two-run home run, leading the Cardinals to a 5-2 victory and on to the World Series. Pujols's lifetime dream was about to become a reality. "This is what you dream about, going to the World Series as a little boy," he said, quoted in *Albert the Great*. "Getting the opportunity to play Game 7 against the best pitcher in baseball

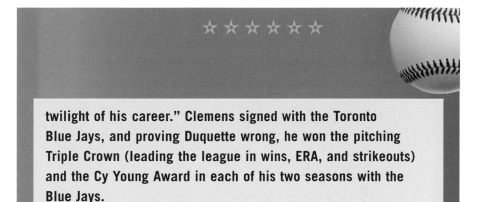

twilight of his career." Clemens signed with the Toronto Blue Jays, and proving Duquette wrong, he won the pitching Triple Crown (leading the league in wins, ERA, and strikeouts) and the Cy Young Award in each of his two seasons with the Blue Jays.

He was traded to the New York Yankees for the 1999 season and had his first World Series success when the Yankees became world champions in 1999 and 2000. In 2001, Clemens became the first pitcher to start a season 20–1. He finished the year at 20–3.

He won his 300th game in 2003, an astounding accomplishment for a modern pitcher, and he is one of just four pitchers to have more than 4,000 strikeouts. From 2004 to 2006, he pitched for the Houston Astros. In 2007, Clemens signed a one-year deal worth $28 million to play again for the New York Yankees. On July 2, he recorded his 350th win with a 5-1 victory over the Minnesota Twins. As of the end of the 2007 season, Clemens had compiled a 354–184 record, with 4,664 strikeouts. He is second only to Nolan Ryan in career strikeouts.

for the past 20 years, Roger Clemens, he's amazing. It doesn't get any better than that."

To the surprise of absolutely no one, Pujols was named the MVP of the championship series, with a remarkable .500 batting average, 4 home runs, 9 RBIs, and a record 14 hits in a seven-game postseason series. As always, Pujols was modest about his award, saying that it belonged to everybody on the team. For that reason, he insisted that the trophy would be staying in the team locker room.

Little did the Cardinals know that the series against the Astros would be the climax of their season. Playing against the Boston Red Sox, a team that had not won a World Series since 1918 and was determined to end the curse, the Cardinals lost in four straight games. The much-vaunted Cardinal offense failed to come through, with Scott Rolen going 0-for-15 and Jim Edmonds getting only one hit, a bunt single. Pujols did a bit better, hitting .333 in the Series, but with no home runs or RBIs. And with that, the team's World Series dream ended for another year.

Still, Pujols was proud of what the team had accomplished. After all, at the start of the season, nobody had expected the Cardinals to do better than third place. He was still disappointed, but determined not to let the loss get him down. Instead, Pujols would use the experience to prepare himself for the next season.

Making a Difference

Going into the 2005 season, the Cardinals, based on their record of the previous year, were the odds-on favorites to repeat as the National League pennant winners. And while Albert Pujols as usual prepared himself physically and mentally for another season and another possible run at the World Series, he had more on his mind than baseball.

For years, ever since he had met Deidre and Isabella, Pujols had worked hard to raise money for and increase awareness of Down syndrome. For example, before a game in September 2002, a 10-year-old girl with Down syndrome, Kathleen Mertz of Lake St. Louis, Missouri, was asked to throw out the ceremonial first ball. Pujols acted as her catcher and then signed her shirt while the two talked. "I could see her talking to him, and she was acting like she was swinging the bat," Tracey Mertz,

DEIDRE PUJOLS

Albert and Deidre Pujols announced the establishment of the Pujols Family Foundation during a news conference on May 5, 2005, in St. Louis. The foundation's mission is to help people with Down syndrome and their families as well as to assist the poor in the Dominican Republic.

Kathleen's mother, told the *St. Louis Post-Dispatch*. "She yelled, 'Hey Albert, hit me a home run.'" Pujols smiled, nodded, and in the first inning, with two runners on base, hit a three-run home run.

Events like that were nice. But now in 2005, backed by enormous celebrity and with the financial means to do so, Pujols felt the need to do more.

Having grown up poor in the Dominican Republic, Pujols keenly felt the need to give to those who do not have and to remember what it is like not to have. It is said that he does not get carried away with personal spending, preferring to live in a relatively modest home rather than a huge mansion. "I grew up poor. I never forgot where I came from," he said, quoted in Jeff Savage's *Albert Pujols*. "It makes you feel good inside to remember."

For Albert and Deidre Pujols, remembering means giving back to the community, helping those in need. It is a strong part of who they are and of their religious beliefs. Pujols has participated as often as he can in charity events and in work with organizations like the Make-A-Wish Foundation. It is reported that he donates 10 to 20 percent of his salary to the Kansas City Baptist Temple, which he and his family attend. Still, he and Deidre wanted to do more.

So on May 5, 2005 (5/5/05—No. 5 is Pujols's number), they launched the Pujols Family Foundation, which is dedicated to "the love, care, and development of people with Down syndrome and their families," as well as to helping the poor in the Dominican Republic. The foundation's Web site records its mission statement:

> To live and share our commitment to faith, family and others.
>
> The Pujols Family Foundation was founded in 2005 with the sole purpose of reflecting the love and compassion for children in the hearts of Albert and Deidre Pujols. We are committed to a calling of love and service, dedicating our lives to seeing every child as God's creation—more precious and important to Him than anyone could ever imagine.
>
> At the core of the Pujols Family Foundation is the belief that every person is special in the sight of God. Albert and Deidre . . . all have a heart for faith, family, and others. Each

has been blessed with different talents and abilities that come together to create a team that is greater than the sum of its parts.

As Albert Pujols said at the press conference announcing the establishment of the foundation, "I want to hit a grand slam off the field. It wasn't something we started on our own; it was something that God showed us."

From helping to sponsor baseball leagues for children with special needs to assisting families who have children with Down syndrome to sending badly needed school supplies, dentists, and dental equipment to villages in the Dominican Republic, the Pujols Family Foundation has begun to make a difference in people's lives.

In addition, Pujols participates in events like the Albert Pujols Celebrity Golf Classic to help raise money for the Down Syndrome Foundation as well as the Pujols Family Foundation. As he says on the foundation's Web site, "This is what it's all about. God gave me an opportunity, and I feel blessed to take advantage of every opportunity I have." For Albert and Deidre, baseball and the celebrity it brings are only tools to help with their work in the service of God.

When it is time to play baseball, though, Pujols's concentration is unshakable. As the 2005 season began, he was more determined than ever to do what he could to bring the World Series championship home to St. Louis.

THE 2005 SEASON

As in 2004, the Cardinals dominated their division. Despite a shoulder injury to Scott Rolen, the team still finished ahead of its archrivals, the Houston Astros, by 11 games. The team had a new double-play combination, with shortstop David Eckstein and second baseman Mark Grudzielanek taking over for Edgar Rentería and Tony Womack. The Cardinals also added another strong pitching arm with free agent Mark Mulder, who teamed with 21-game winner Chris Carpenter to give the Cardinals a strong one-two punch.

Pujols, too, had an amazing year, once again leading the league with 129 runs scored and crushing 41 homers with 117 RBIs. He also led the Cardinals with 16 stolen bases, impressive for a man of his size, and he demonstrated extraordinary patience at the plate, even without Rolen's protection, walking a career-high 97 times. In the National League batting race, Pujols lost to Chicago first baseman Derrek Lee in a squeaker, .335 to .330.

In their first postseason matchup, the Cardinals defeated the San Diego Padres in a three-game sweep. Pujols once again was stellar, hitting .556 and drawing three intentional walks.

Now, the only team that stood between the Cardinals and a return to the World Series was the Houston Astros, who had made the postseason as the wild-card team. The Cardinals won the first game, but Astro pitching dominated the next three games of the series, with starting pitchers Roy Oswalt and Roger Clemens getting victories.

St. Louis needed to win Game 5 to fend off elimination, but with the Astros leading 4-2 in the ninth inning, it looked as if the Cardinals' chances were nearly over.

Down to their last out and strike and facing elimination with the Astros' shutdown closer Brad Lidge throwing nearly unhittable breaking pitches, David Eckstein gave hope to the Cardinals, hitting a single in the hole on the left side to reach first base. The tying run was at the plate, and that batter, Jim Edmonds, managed a walk. Then, with two out and two on, Pujols stepped up to the plate. The team's fate was in his hands.

After one strike, Pujols slammed what can only be called a towering drive 412 feet (125 meters) onto the train tracks

Albert Pujols is about to connect on a three-run homer in Game 5 of the 2005 National League Championship Series against the Astros. With the hit, coming with two outs in the ninth inning, the Cardinals staved off elimination in the series. The Astros, though, would win the next game and the pennant.

behind left field. If the game had been played with the roof open, the drive would have exited Minute Maid Park, as it first hit off the glass wall that forms part of the roof. The Cardinals were ahead, 5-4. In an instant, the roar of the Astros' home crowd turned into stunned silence, and the Cardinals held on for the win, forcing a sixth game.

Unfortunately for the Cardinals, Astro pitcher Roy Oswalt was untouchable in Game 6, and the Astros celebrated their first pennant in the final game at Busch Stadium in St. Louis. (The Cardinals would move to the new Busch Stadium for the 2006 season.) Once again, the Cardinals' hopes to play in the World Series were dashed.

Despite the letdown of having to watch the World Series at home that fall, Pujols had had yet another season to remember. His reputation as one of baseball's true superstars was enhanced when he was named, for the first time, the National League's Most Valuable Player.

"I'm going to celebrate tonight," Pujols said, after learning about the award. "It's an honor. But I still need that [World Series] ring. That's my next dream."

Earlier in the season, Pujols was chosen to be pictured on Wheaties cereal boxes—an honor for America's sports heroes. Pujols had this to say when the new cereal box was unveiled at Busch Stadium on April 7, 2005. "I'm pretty sure my kids are going to be looking at me, too. . . . They're going to be saying, 'I want Daddy's cereal.' It's like winning an MVP award. . . . There are lots of great players out there that Wheaties could have picked, and they chose me. It's an honor. It's a great day!"

Although honor after honor was showered upon Pujols, one event in 2005 stood out and was more important than any other. On November 5, 2005, Albert and Deidre's daughter, Sophia Adela Pujols, was born. Albert could not have been happier, nor could his year have had a better ending. In a letter posted on his family foundation's Web site, Albert expressed his feelings about 2005:

> On May 5th, 2005, we launched our Family Foundation. I knew in my heart that this is something that God called Dee

☆ ☆ ☆ ☆ ☆

WHEATIES

Wheaties is a popular breakfast cereal that was introduced in 1924 by the General Mills cereal company. Since 1933, it has been associated with sports and athletes and is known for its slogan, "The Breakfast of Champions."

Throughout the 1930s, Wheaties increased in popularity with its sponsorship of radio broadcasts of baseball games. During these events, testimonials from athletes were used to demonstrate that Wheaties was indeed the breakfast of champions. Since 1934, the best athletes of the time have been depicted on Wheaties packaging, a tradition that continues to this day.

Lou Gehrig was the first athlete whose picture was used on a Wheaties box in 1934. Since then, great athletes like Babe Didrikson and Lee Trevino, Mary Lou Retton and Walter Payton, Michael Jordan and Tiger Woods, and of course Albert Pujols have all made appearances on the cereal box. The 1987 Minnesota Twins, the World Series champions that year, were the first team to appear on the box. Michael Jordan has appeared on the Wheaties box 18 times—more than any other athlete. Next is Tiger Woods, with 14 appearances.

It is considered an honor, a recognition of an athlete's extraordinary talent and popularity to be selected by Wheaties. It says to the athlete, "You've made it."

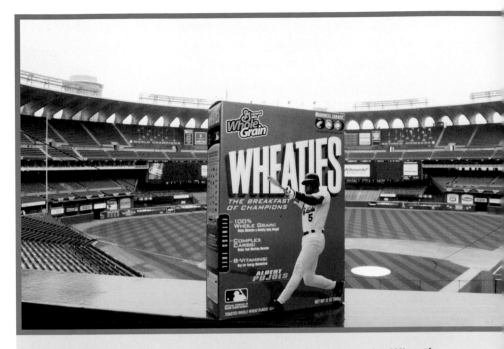

Albert Pujols was chosen in April 2005 to be pictured on the Wheaties cereal box, shown here in Busch Stadium in St. Louis. "It's like winning an MVP award," Pujols said about the honor. Later that year, Pujols would really find out what winning the MVP award was like.

Dee (Deidre) and me to do. However, I never had any idea how many blessings would come our way as a result of simply being obedient to His call.

In 2005 Dee Dee and I not only shared in the birth of our charitable foundation but also in the birth of our beautiful daughter, Sophia. God also blessed me with good health and a productive year that brought my first National League MVP award.

Even though 2005 was one of the most rewarding years of my life, I must look forward and see all the new and wonderful things that our foundation will accomplish in the future. I know that 2006 will be even greater than 2005!

Albert Pujols was living a storybook existence. He had a beautiful wife and children. He was at the top of his game as a baseball player. And, because of his success as an athlete, he was in a position, through his foundation, to lend assistance to those most in need. In the next year, Pujols faced a year of ups and downs, including one more attempt at the World Series, and the first physical signs that he is, indeed, human.

10

Winning It All

With the start of the 2006 season, the Cardinals, led by Albert Pujols, were more determined than ever to win the world championship for St. Louis. And playing for the first time in the new Busch Stadium, Pujols was as focused as he had ever been on winning the championship for himself, for his team, and for his fans.

Because the fans in St. Louis had always given him so much support, he wanted to win for them the championship they deserved. As he said, quoted on the *Baseball Almanac* Web site, "This is a great city to play [in]. Anywhere you go, you're going to have great fans, but not like you have here in St. Louis. I've only played in St. Louis. I haven't played anywhere else, but even when the other teams come here they tell us, 'Man, I can't believe how nice the fans are here.' . . . We've got the best fans.

A lot of people want to come and play in St. Louis because of the way the fans treat us."

Always supremely confident about his abilities as a hitter, Pujols was becoming just as confident as a fielder. Since the 2004 season, Pujols had stopped moving from position to position, finally becoming the team's full-time first baseman. By 2005, John Dewan had noted in *The Fielding Bible* that no first baseman was better at digging balls out of the dirt than Pujols. In fact, Pujols saved 42 bad throws by his fielders in 2005; Derrek Lee was second with 23.

THE SEASON BEGINS

Along with the New York Mets, the Cardinals had the National League's best top-to-bottom lineup. They had a strong pitching staff led by Chris Carpenter, who had won the National League Cy Young Award in 2005. Hopes were high for another strong season.

The team got off to an auspicious start in its new home on April 10, 2006, with a 6-4 victory over the Milwaukee Brewers. April belonged to the Cardinals and Pujols, who hit 14 home runs for the month, a new major-league record, breaking the old mark of 13 set by Luis González and Ken Griffey, Jr. By the end of May, he had 25 home runs and 65 RBIs, was already being discussed as the league MVP, and was on pace to beat Barry Bonds' home-run record of 73 set in 2001. The team itself had gotten off to a blistering 31–16 start. It looked as if all systems were a go for another record-breaking season for the team and for Pujols. One bad strain, though, would threaten the remainder of his and the Cardinals' seasons.

ON THE DL

On Saturday, June 3, 2006, Pujols was chasing a foul ball off the bat of Cubs third baseman Aramis Ramírez when he felt a sharp pain in his side. The injury, diagnosed as a strained right

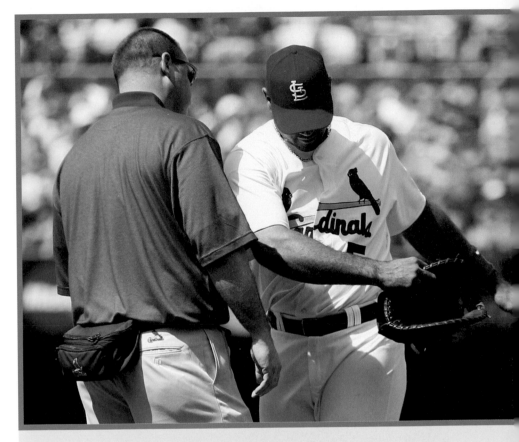

Greg Hauck, an assistant trainer with the Cardinals, examined Albert Pujols after Pujols pulled up lame while chasing a foul ball during a game on June 3, 2006. Pujols strained his right oblique muscle and was placed on the disabled list for the first time in his career.

oblique muscle, put him on the disabled list for the first time in his career. It was predicted that he could be sidelined from 15 days up to six weeks.

At first it looked likely that he could miss a good part of the season. John Adams, who had spent 24 years as a trainer for the Milwaukee Brewers and the Montreal Expos, told *USA Today*, "When you see those things, you're looking at a minimum of four weeks. I don't want to pigeonhole him, but under normal recovery, it's a thing where you can cross out the month of June, and maybe the All-Star Game, too."

The Cardinals, as much as they needed Pujols in the lineup, were determined not to rush him back. "If you send the guy out there too early, then you have a major setback and a major reinjury," George Paletta, the Cardinals' team doctor, told reporters, quoted in *USA Today*. "This is not an injury that he can go out and play with it sore, because that will put him at risk. He can't play at 60 or 70 percent."

Pujols, though, was determined to return as quickly as he was able and was certain that he would be playing sooner rather than later. As he said in a June 7 letter to his fans, posted on the family foundation Web site:

> Thank you everyone for your well wishes and your concern since my injury. . . . I feel good. I am feeling a little stronger each day. The doctors and trainers are watching my progress daily. I am listening to them. I am taking it easy, and I'm not trying to overdo it right now. Although the doctors and trainers will tell me when I am ready to play again, I know that it will be God's touch that will restore my strength!
>
> Thank you for all your cards, letters and e-mails. But, most of all, thank you for your prayers! I know my strength comes from Christ, and my healing in Him too. Please continue to pray for me as I trust his perfect timing in my recovery.

This note clearly shows his close relationship with his fans, as well as his deep religious faith and trust in God.

Some had actually predicted that Pujols could be on the disabled list for up to eight weeks. Helped in no small part by his strenuous off-season training routine, which keeps him in prime physical condition, he returned to the lineup on June 22.

In his second game back, he went 4-for-4 at the plate, letting the world know that he had returned.

As the season progressed, injuries took their toll on other Cardinal players. Pitcher Jason Isringhausen was out for the year, and center fielder Jim Edmonds and shortstop David Eckstein also lost significant time.

Because of these injuries, the team struggled through the remainder of the regular season. In late June, the Cardinals suffered an eight-game losing streak. Another eight-game losing streak occurred from July 27 to August 4. Then, in late September, with a lead of seven games over the Cincinnati Reds and eight-and-a-half games over the Houston Astros, the Cardinals lost seven straight games, and the Astros won nine straight.

St. Louis's lead in the division shrank to only a half game. It was nearly the worst collapse in baseball history, but on the last day of the season, despite a 5-3 loss to the Milwaukee Brewers, the Cardinals clinched the National League Central Division title when the Astros also lost, 3-1, to Atlanta. The Cardinals ended the season with a record of 83–78, the third-worst ever for a team in the play-offs, and they were considered unlikely to advance past the first round.

It is improbable that the Cardinals would have even made it that far without Pujols. Despite not playing a full season because of his injury, he still posted career highs with 49 home runs, 137 RBIs, and a .671 slugging average. He was now the first player in major-league history to hit 30 or more home runs in each of his first six seasons. If the Cardinals had not faded in the homestretch, it is likely that he would have won his second MVP award, which went instead to Ryan Howard of the Philadelphia Phillies.

One of his proudest accomplishments of the 2006 season occurred during a game against Pittsburgh in early September. There, with thousands of children with Down syndrome cheering him on (they were there as part of the Buddy Walk charity that Pujols has chaired since 2002), he hit three home runs in a single game. It was his second three-homer day of the season.

Not only was he one of baseball's premier hitters, but he also received recognition in 2006 for his fielding skills, earning his first Gold Glove award. He was now a complete ballplayer, lacking only speed to make him totally unbeatable.

POSTSEASON

When the play-offs began, everyone on the team (with the exception of the closer Isringhausen) was healthy and back in the lineup. Still, no other team in baseball history had won the championship after so few wins in the regular season. The Cardinals, despite their air of confidence, would have their work cut out for them.

Pujols was determined that their weak record would not stop them from going all the way. As he said, "You don't play to win the division, you play to win championship rings. . . . How many division titles does this team have? We don't care about that. It doesn't matter what record we have. [In 2004,] we had the best record in the majors and we lost in the World Series."

Once again, the Cardinals easily defeated the San Diego Padres in the National League Division Series, with Pujols going 5-for-8 in the first two games. Going into the National League Championship Series as heavy underdogs, the Cardinals beat the New York Mets in seven exciting games. The Mets pitched around Pujols as much as possible (he still batted 7-for-22), which left the heroics to players like pitcher Jeff Suppan and catcher Yadier Molina, who delivered the pennant-winning home run in the ninth inning of Game 7 at Shea Stadium in New York. The Cardinals were now set to meet the Detroit Tigers in the World Series.

According to most observers, the Cardinals did not stand a chance against Detroit. As Bob Nightengale predicted in *USA*

Today, "The Detroit Tigers' biggest obstacle to a championship will be keeping a straight face. The Tigers in three. (OK, make it four.)" In the same article, a baseball scout said, "To me, the National League doesn't have a prayer. The Tigers are hot, exquisitely managed, and have the home-field advantage."

Sometimes, though, events do not turn out quite as predicted. Pujols had had a relatively quiet postseason, batting "only" .324 and hampered by a nagging hamstring injury. Tiger manager Jim Leyland was faced with a decision: Pitch to Pujols or not?

In Game 1 of the Series, Leyland decided to pitch to him. After striking out in the first inning, Pujols came to bat in the third inning and smashed a two-run homer into the right-field seats, knocking the heart out of the Tigers and their fans and propelling the Cardinals to a 7-2 win. Questioned later about his decision to challenge Pujols, Leyland said, quoted in *Cardinals Rule*, "I could go into a lot of detail about that, but I'll leave it at this: The manager's decision is either to pitch to him or walk him. I pitched to him, and obviously he burned us." As Pujols said modestly, "I just go out there and just try to see the ball, and put a good swing [on it]."

After the Tigers won the second game of the Series in Detroit, the teams moved to St. Louis. There, the Cardinals swept the hapless Tigers, who were plagued by fielding errors and an inability to get the big hits when they needed them.

Pujols hit only .200 in the Series, with a double, a home run, and five walks. Still, without him, it is highly unlikely that the Cardinals would ever have made it to the Series in the first place. As for Pujols, he was thrilled that the chase, for now, was over. His team had won the world championship. As he said, quoted in Jeff Savage's *Albert Pujols*, "Now I can say I have a Series ring in my trophy case. And that's what you play for." In the past, Pujols had said that he would happily trade his MVP award for a World Series ring. Now he had both.

With his son, A.J., on his shoulders, Albert Pujols held up the World Series trophy along with Cardinals manager Tony La Russa. St. Louis defeated the Detroit Tigers, four games to one, to win the 2006 World Series. Standing behind the trophy was Walt Jocketty, the Cardinals' general manager.

WHAT'S NEXT

As Pujols looked forward to the 2007 season and the possibility of another World Series ring, he had much to occupy his time. In January 2007, he led a humanitarian mission to his native Dominican Republic, bringing medicine, health care, and health advice to 1,000 children in three poor villages. Pujols missed the Cardinals' visit to the White House in order to make the trip.

As he said on his Web site:

This is a trip that we've been planning for almost a year. I'm taking six doctors and two assistants down to the Dominican [Republic]. As of right now, we have three villages that we're going to work on, and we've got 1,000 kids that we're going to work with in six days. The doctors are ready to go. . . .

I'm looking forward to it. This is something that's going to be a really good experience for me, for my family, and for the foundation. For the doctors, they don't know what they're going to face. I know what they're going to face. People that are poor, they've never seen TVs before. Some of the villages, if it rains, we probably won't be able to get there because it gets flooded. But I'm looking forward to it, and I think it's going to be a great experience.

The mission had a wide range of aims. One goal was health education and helping to improve hygiene. If possible, children who needed surgery would be transported to the United States to receive treatment.

Pujols gives of himself in other ways. Fundraising, personal appearances, celebrity golf tournaments—anything he can do to raise money and help those who need assistance. Pujols also enjoys giving advice to young Latin American baseball players. As he said, quoted in Jeff Savage's *Albert Pujols,* "I know how tough it is to come here knowing no English. You don't need to give money to these kids. You just need to encourage them to keep working hard and take advantage of the opportunities they get."

Coming to the United States as a young man searching for a better life, Pujols was well aware of the opportunities that this country can offer. As a kind of "thank you" to his adopted country, on February 7, 2007, Albert Pujols became a U.S. citizen.

He had studied for more than a year, tutored by his wife, Deidre, to prepare himself for the citizenship exam. "He even answered a bunch of additional questions and gave us more answers than we asked," Chester Moyer, the officer in charge of the U.S. Citizenship and Immigration Services office in St. Louis, said, quoted by The Associated Press. "He clenched his fist and said, 'I got 100 percent!' He was thrilled to become a citizen."

☆ ☆ ☆ ☆ ☆

THE BUDDY WALK

Since 1995, the Buddy Walk has become one of the premier advocacy events for Down syndrome and has become an important occasion in communities throughout the country.

The National Down Syndrome Society established the Buddy Walk to celebrate Down Syndrome Awareness Month in October. In its first year, Buddy Walks took place in 17 locations across the United States.

The Buddy Walk has three main goals: to promote the acceptance and inclusion of people with Down syndrome; to raise funds locally and nationally for education, research, and advocacy programs; and to enhance the position of the Down syndrome community, enabling people to influence local and national policy and practice.

In 2006, more than 260 Buddy Walks were held across the country and abroad, raising about $6.5 million for sponsoring Buddy Walk organizations and the National Down Syndrome Society. More than 250,000 people are expected to participate in a Buddy Walk in 2007. Altogether since its inception in 1995, more than 1,750,000 people have participated in the program. Maybe you can help organize or take part in one in your own community. To learn more, visit http://www.buddywalk.org.

Albert Pujols had his picture taken with Stephanie Schecter before a game against the Cincinnati Reds on June 6, 2007, at Busch Stadium. Several Cardinals and Reds players met with a group of teenagers and adults with Down syndrome as part of the Buses for Baseball program sponsored by the Major League Baseball Players Trust. Pujols has been active for years in raising money and awareness for Down syndrome organizations.

And, of course, most important to Pujols is the time he spends with his family. The Pujolses live as close to a normal life as the family of a sports superstar can live, going out for pizza or to the movies on family nights. Pujols reads to Isabella, A.J., and Sophia every night. As he has constantly said, God and family are the most important things in his life, the things that really matter to him.

HEADING INTO 2007

As baseball's premier hitter, he is not going to quit anytime soon. His drive to be the best and to bring more championships back home to St. Louis will not let him rest on his considerable laurels. Going into the 2007 season, he was optimistic about his health.

"I took a month and a half off to make sure I don't try to come back too soon," he said on the foundation Web site. "I'd rather be greedy later on than early when I'm working out. I feel good so far, knock on wood. I haven't felt any of those injuries that I suffered during the [2006] season, and that's a good sign, but you can't tell until you start doing a lot of baseball stuff, taking ground balls every day and swinging every day."

Although Pujols was optimistic heading into the 2007 season, he got off to a very slow start. Just the year before, in 2006, he had set a major-league record with 14 home runs for the month of April. In 2007, he hit only six homers, with 15 RBIs. His batting average was, for him, a relatively dismal .250

The Cardinals themselves were faring little better. They finished the month of April at the bottom of the standings in the National League Central Division with a record of just 10–14. Bad news haunted the team, when, on April 29, relief pitcher Josh Hancock was killed in a car accident, the second Cardinals pitcher to die in five seasons. The team struggled for the remainder of the year, ultimately finishing out of the playoff picture, in third place in the National League Central with a record of 78–84.

While the team failed in its attempt to repeat as World Series champions, Pujols found his rhythm as the season progressed. As April turned to May, and the weather got hotter, so did Pujols's bat. For the month of May, he batted .340, although he hit only three homers. His batting gradually improved throughout the first half of the season, until by the time of the All-Star break, he was hitting .310 with a .516 slugging percentage and 52 RBIs.

After the break, the Pujols of the previous six seasons broke through, as he hit four home runs in his first three games back against the Philadelphia Phillies. Pujols was also named Player of the Week for the week of July 9 to 15, after hitting a blistering 9-for-15 with a 1.357 slugging percentage and 19 total bases. He slammed his twenty-fifth home run on August 15, making him just the fifth player in major-league history to hit 25 home runs in his first seven seasons.

Just one week later, after hitting a home run in five straight games, Pujols added to his own legend by becoming the first major-league player ever to hit 30 home runs in each of his first seven seasons. By the end of the season, Pujols was hitting .327, with a slugging percentage of .568. He finished the year with 32 home runs and 103 RBIs.

Only 28 years old, there is no telling how high he can go. He has more home runs and RBIs than Hank Aaron did at his age, has scored more runs than Rickey Henderson did at his age, has more hits than Pete Rose did at his age. If he stays healthy, it is amazing to think of the number of records he is capable of breaking. With luck, Pujols could go down as baseball's greatest all-around player. Even if he doesn't, he will still be one of baseball's true superstars, a good teammate and team leader, a gentleman and family man famous for his accomplishments both on and off the field.

STATISTICS

ALBERT PUJOLS

Primary position: First base
(Also 3B; LF; RF)

Full name: José Alberto Pujols •
Born: January 16, 1980, Santo
Domingo, Dominican Republic •
Height: 6'3" Weight: 210 lbs. • Teams:
(St. Louis Cardinals, 2001–present)

YEAR	TEAM	G	AB	H	HR	RBI	BA
2001	STL	161	590	194	37	130	.329
2002	STL	157	590	185	34	127	.314
2003	STL	157	591	212	43	124	.359
2004	STL	154	592	196	46	123	.331
2005	STL	161	591	195	41	117	.330
2006	STL	143	535	177	49	137	.331
2007	STL	158	565	185	32	103	.327
TOTAL		1,091	4,054	1,344	282	861	.332

KEY: STL = St. Louis Cardinals; G = Games; AB = At-bats; H = Hits; HR = Home runs;
RBI = Runs batted in; BA = Batting average

CHRONOLOGY

1980 **January 16** Born José Alberto Pujols in Santo Domingo, Dominican Republic.

1996 The Pujols family emigrates from the Dominican Republic to the United States, ultimately settling in Independence, Missouri.

1998 Meets 21-year-old Deidre "Dee Dee" Corona, a single mother of two-month-old Isabella, who was born with Down syndrome; the two quickly fall in love.

1999 Noticed by major-league scouts while playing for Maple Woods Community College; drafted in the thirteenth round by the St. Louis Cardinals.

2000 **January 1** Albert and Deidre marry.

Plays Class A ball with the Peoria Chiefs and then spends a month with the Potomac Cannons; is promoted to the Class AAA Memphis Redbirds and is named MVP of the Pacific Coast League championships.

2001 Son Albert Pujols, Jr., better known as A.J., is born; earns place on the St. Louis Cardinals roster after just one season in the minors; named National League Rookie of the Year.

2002 Finishes second in voting for National League Most Valuable Player, hitting .314 with 34 home runs.

2003 Again finishes second in voting for National League Most Valuable Player; bats .359 and wins National League batting title.

2004 Signs a seven-year, $100 million contract with the Cardinals; bats .331 with 46 home runs; named Most Valuable Player of the National League Championship

Series against the Houston Astros; the Cardinals lose the World Series in four games to the Boston Red Sox.

2005   **May 5** Albert and Deidre Pujols establish the Pujols Family Foundation, dedicated to helping people with Down syndrome and their families, as well as assisting the poor in the Dominican Republic.

Wins National League Most Valuable Player award after a season in which he bats .330, scores 129 runs, and hits 41 home runs with 117 RBIs.

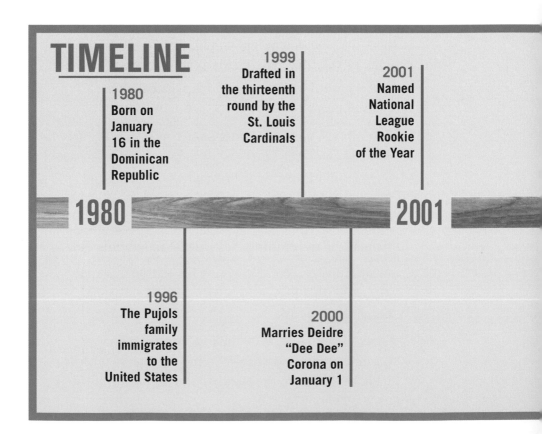

TIMELINE

1999
Drafted in the thirteenth round by the St. Louis Cardinals

2001
Named National League Rookie of the Year

1980
Born on January 16 in the Dominican Republic

1980

2001

1996
The Pujols family immigrates to the United States

2000
Marries Deidre "Dee Dee" Corona on January 1

November 5 Daughter Sophia is born.

2006   Hits a career-high 49 home runs with 137 RBIs; receives his first Gold Glove award for his fielding at first base; the Cardinals win the World Series, defeating the Detroit Tigers in five games.

2007   **February 7** Becomes a U.S. citizen.

Becomes the first player in major-league history to hit more than 30 home runs in each of his first seven seasons.

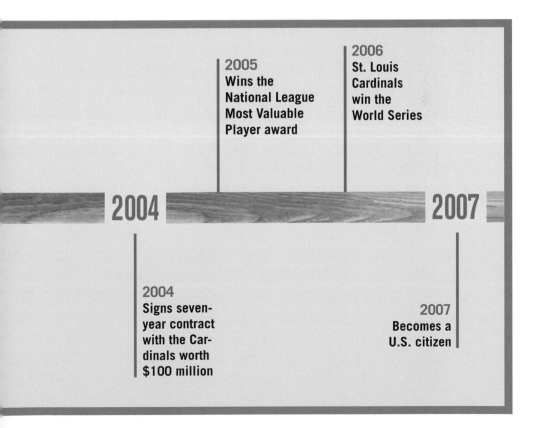

2005
Wins the
National League
Most Valuable
Player award

2006
St. Louis
Cardinals
win the
World Series

2004

2007

2004
Signs seven-
year contract
with the Car-
dinals worth
$100 million

2007
Becomes a
U.S. citizen

GLOSSARY

All-Star team A team for each league, consisting of the season's best players as voted on by the fans. The All-Star Game takes place in mid-July, symbolizing the "halfway point" of the major-league season.

assist The official scorer awards an assist to every defensive player who fields or touches the ball (after it is hit by the batter) before a putout.

at-bat An official turn at batting that is charged to a baseball player, except when the player walks, sacrifices, is hit by a pitched ball, or is interfered with by a catcher. At-bats are used to calculate a player's batting average and slugging percentage.

ball A pitch that does not pass over home plate in the strike zone. A batter who receives four balls gets a walk.

base on balls The awarding of first base to a batter after a pitcher throws four balls. Also known as a walk, it is "intentional" when the four balls are thrown on purpose to avoid pitching to a batter.

batter's box The area to the left and right of home plate in which the batter must be standing for fair play to take place.

batting average The number of hits a batter gets divided by the number of times the player is at bat. For example, 3 hits in 10 at-bats would be a .300 batting average.

catcher The player who crouches behind home plate and signals to the pitcher what type of pitch to throw. This player also catches the pitches the batter misses or does not swing at, as well as covers home plate during defensive plays.

cleanup hitter The fourth batter in the lineup, usually a power hitter. The team hopes runners are on base for the "cleanup" hitter to drive home. Ideally, the first three batters of the game would get on base, so that the fourth batter could "clean up" the bases with a grand slam.

closer   A relief pitcher who is consistently used to "close" or finish the game by getting the final outs.

contract   A binding written agreement. In baseball, a player signs a contract that establishes his salary for a set number of years to play for a particular team.

cross-checker   A veteran scout for a team who looks at prospects recommended by local scouts.

double   A hit that gets the batter to second base without the aid of a fielding error.

doubleheader   Two baseball games played by the same teams on the same day.

Down syndrome   A condition at birth that causes slowed growth, distinctive physical characteristics, and some degree of mental retardation.

draft   Major League Baseball's mechanism for assigning amateur players to its teams. The draft order is determined based on the previous season's standings, with the team with the worst record receiving the first pick.

earned run average   The number of earned runs that a pitcher allows every nine innings. It is computed by multiplying the total number of earned runs by nine and dividing by the number of innings pitched.

error   When a defensive player makes a mistake that results in a runner reaching base or advancing a base, an error is designated by the game's scorer.

farm team   A team that provides training and experience for young players, with the expectation that successful players will move to the major leagues.

grand slam   A home run that is hit when the bases are loaded.

home run   When a batter hits a ball into the stands in fair territory, it is a home run. The batter may also have an inside-the-park home run if the ball never leaves the playing field and the runner is able to reach home plate without stopping before being tagged by a defensive player. A home run counts as one run, and if there are any runners on base when a home run is hit, they too score.

inning   The time during which both teams have come to bat and each has made three outs. The top of an inning is when the visiting team comes to bat, and the bottom of an inning is when the home team comes to bat. In professional baseball, a standard game is nine innings. In college baseball, it may be seven or nine. In Little League, it may be three to six innings.

lineup   A list that is presented to the umpire and opposing coach before the start of the game that contains the order in which the batters will bat as well as the defensive fielding positions they will play.

MVP   The Most Valuable Player award (commonly known as the MVP) is an annual award given to one outstanding player in each league (American and National) of Major League Baseball. The award is determined by the Baseball Writers' Association of America.

oblique muscles   The thin, flat muscles that form the middle and outer layers of the side walls of the abdomen.

on deck   The offensive player next in line to bat after the current batter is said to be on deck. Often the player on deck will swing a weighted bat to warm up and stay in an area called the on-deck circle.

pull the ball   To hit the ball hard with a full swing toward the natural side of the field. A right-handed hitter pulls the ball to the left side of the field; a left-handed batter, to the right side.

RBI   A run batted in is generally given to a batter for each run scored as the result of his appearance at the plate.

single   A hit that gets the batter to first base without the aid of a fielding error.

strike   A pitch that is swung at and missed or a pitch that is in the strike zone and is not swung at. A foul ball counts as a strike unless it would be the third strike. Three strikes and the batter is out.

sweet spot   The area around the center mass of the bat that is the most effective part with which to hit a ball.

triple   A hit that gets the batter to third base without the aid of a fielding error.

triple play   When three outs are made on one play. The occurrence is very rare.

walk-off home run   A game-ending home run by the home team—so named because the losing team has to walk off the field.

World Series   The championship series of Major League Baseball. The Series is played between the pennant winners of the American League and the National League in a best-of-seven play-off.

BIBLIOGRAPHY

"Albert Pujols." Wikipedia. Available online at http://en.wikipedia.org/wiki/Albert_Pujols.

"Albert Pujols Baseball Stats." *Baseball Almanac.* Available online at http://www.baseball-almanac.com/players/player. php?p=pujols101.

"Albert Pujols Biography." *JockBio.com.* Available online at http://www.jockbio.com/Bios/Pujols/Pujols_bio.html.

"Barry Bonds." *Wikipedia.* Available online at http://en.wikipedia.org/wiki/Barry_Bonds.

"Baseball, a National Passion." *DominicanRepublic.com.* Available online at http://www.dominicanrepublic.com/ theculture/baseball.php.

Cardinals Rule. Associated Press. Chicago: Triumph Books, 2006.

"Darryl Kile." *Wikipedia.* Available online at http://en.wikipedia.org/wiki/Darryl_Kile.

"Dominican American." *Wikipedia.* Available online at http://en.wikipedia.org/wiki/Dominican_American.

"Dominican Republic Pastimes, Baseball, Béisbol." *Colonial Zone Dominican Republic.* Available online at http://www.colonialzone-dr.com/pastimes-baseball.html.

"Dominican Winter Baseball League." *Wikipedia.* Available online at http://en.wikipedia.org/wiki/Dominican_ Winter_Baseball_League.

Edes, Gordon. "One That Got Away." *Boston Globe.* October 11, 2006. Available online at http://www.boston.com/sports/ redsox/articles/2006/10/11/one_that_got_away.

Fadem, Susan. "Swinging for the Fences." *St. Louis Woman Magazine.* April 2006. Available online at http://www. stlouiswomanmag.com/covergallery/06/apr.html.

Habib, Daniel G. "A Swing of Beauty." *Sports Illustrated.*
May 22, 2006. Available online at http://sportsillustrated.
cnn.com/2006/magazine/06/09/pujols0522/index.html.

Homeier, Barbara P., and Charles I. Scott. "Down Syndrome."
KidsHealth. Available online at http://www.kidshealth.org/
kid/health_problems/birth_defect/down_syndrome.html.

"Home Run Derby." *Wikipedia.* Available online at
http://en.wikipedia.org/wiki/Home_Run_Derby.

Lewin, Josh. *You Never Forget Your First: Ballplayers
Recall Their Big League Debuts.* Dulles, Virginia: Potomac
Books, 2005.

McHale, Matt. "Albert Pujols: Quickly Becoming Baseball's
Biggest Star." *Baseball Digest.* October 2003. Available online
at http://findarticles.com/p/articles/mi_m0FCI/is_10_62/
ai_107488939.

Merron, Jeff. "The List: Baseball's One-Hit Wonders."
ESPN.com. Available online at http://espn.go.com/page2/list/
onehitwonders.html.

"Minor League Baseball." *Wikipedia.* Available online at
http://en.wikipedia.org/wiki/Minor_league_baseball.

National Down Syndrome Society/Buddy Walk. Available
online at http://www.buddywalk.org.

Nightengale, Bob. "Cardinals' Pujols Lands On Disabled List."
USA Today. June 5, 2006. Available online at http://
www.usatoday.com/sports/baseball/nl/cardinals/
2006-06-04-pujols-dl_x.htm.

———. "World Series Scouting Report: Detroit Tigers," *USA
Today.* October 20, 2006. Available online
at http://www.usatoday.com/sports/baseball/playoffs/
2006-10-20-tigers-scouting-report_x.htm.

"Pujols Becomes U.S. Citizen." *Houston Chronicle.* February 9,
2007.

Pujols Family Foundation: Faith, Family and Others. Available online at http://www.pujolsfamilyfoundation.org.

Quinn, Kay. "Deidre Pujols Talks About Famous Husband, Faith, and Foundation to Help Others." KSDK NewsChannel 5. Available online at http://www.kdsk.com/news/news_article.aspx?storyid=96299.

Rains, Rob. *Albert the Great: The Albert Pujols Story.* Champaign, Ill.: Sports Publishing LLC, 2005.

"Roberto Clemente." *Wikipedia.* Available online at http://en.wikipedia.org/wiki/Roberto_Clemente.

Robinson, Jon. "Albert Pujols Interview: Backyard Baseball, Line Drives, and the Art of Silencing a Crowd." *IGN.com.* May 19, 2006. Available online at http://sports.ign.com/articles/709/709384p1.html.

"Roger Clemens." *Wikipedia.* Available online at http://en.wikipedia.org/wiki/Roger_Clemens.

Savage, Jeff. *Albert Pujols.* Minneapolis, Minn.: Lerner Publications Company, 2007.

"St. Louis Cardinals." *Wikipedia.* Available online at http://en.wikipedia.org/wiki/St._Louis_Cardinals.

Strauss, Joe. "Albert Pujols: Baseball's Most Complete Hitter: Cardinals Slugger Uses His Knowledge, Hard Work, and Ability as a Batsman in Becoming a Dangerous Offensive Force in the Majors." *Baseball Digest.* October 1, 2005. Available online at http://findarticles.com/p/articles/mi_m0FCI/is_6_64/ai_n15340879.

"Wheaties." *Wikipedia.* Available online at http://en.wikipedia.org/wiki/Wheaties.

FURTHER READING

BOOKS

Cardinal Nation: A Celebration of Redbird History.
New York: Sporting News, 2006.

Foley, Erin. *Dominican Republic (Cultures of the World).*
Tarrytown, N.Y.: Marshall Cavendish Corporation, 2005.

Kingsley, Jason, and Mitchell Levitz. *Count Us In:
Growing Up With Down Syndrome.* New York: Harvest
Books, 2007.

Snyder, John. *Cardinals Journal: Year by Year and Day
by Day with the St. Louis Cardinals.* Cincinnati, Ohio:
Emmis Books, 2006.

Wendel, Tim. *The New Face of Baseball: The One-
Hundred-Year Rise and Triumph of Latinos in America's
Favorite Sport.* New York: Rayo, 2003.

WEB SITES

Baseball Almanac
http://www.baseball-almanac.com

Baseball Reference
http://www.baseball-reference.com

National Down Syndrome Society: Buddy Walk
http://www.buddywalk.org

The Official Site of Major League Baseball
http://mlb.mlb.com

Pujols Family Foundation
http://www.pujolsfamilyfoundation.org

PujolsFan.com
http://www.pujolsfan.com

St. Louis Cardinals
http://cardinals.mlb.com

PICTURE CREDITS

INDEX

ABOUT THE AUTHOR

DENNIS ABRAMS is the author of numerous biographies for Chelsea House, including such titles as *Anthony Horowitz, Hamid Karzai, Ty Cobb,* and *Eminem.* He attended Antioch College, where he majored in English and communications, and currently resides in Houston, Texas.

7983